INSTRUCTOR'S
MANUAL
for
HOLISTIC NURSING
A Handbook for Practice

Second Edition

Barbara Montgomery Dossey, RN, MS, HNC, FAAN
Lynn Keegan, RN, PhD, FAAN
Cathie E. Guzzetta, RN, PhD, FAAN
Leslie Gooding Kolkmeier, RN, MEd

An Aspen Publication®
Aspen Publishers, Inc.
Gaithersburg, Maryland
1995

Editorial Resources: Ruth Bloom

ISBN: 0-8342-0705-2

Printed in the United States of America

345

Table of Contents

Introduction

A course in holistic nursing, integrating the art and science of caring and healing, is extraordinary, rewarding, and fulfilling. This is a process course and requires that process strategies be used to present the different topics and modalities. For students to learn the dynamics of health promotion and healing, theory content must be presented in both lecture format and in experiential sessions. It is an opportunity to help students realize what it means to live healthy and inspired lives. It is a journey with students in the exploration of the unity and relatedness of all aspects of living and dying; to awaken the healing potentials within self and others; and to develop and explore different strategies to strengthen the whole person. We invite you and your students to undertake and explore the translation of healing by asking four significant questions:

1. What do you know about the meaning of healing?
2. What can you do each day to facilitate healing in yourself?
3. What is the essence of being a nurse healer?
4. What can you do to enhance your presence of being a nurse healer?

This instructor's manual has been developed to assist in the facilitation and integration of holistic principles. We have offered many strategies. Be creative and add your own personal style to these strategies, guidelines, and suggestions. This course exposes students to the experience of presence and healing. It teaches students different aspects of how to "walk the talk" of holism. The textbook content, chapter format, and teaching methods are designed to nurture the individual student's body, mind, and spirit. The various teaching methods enhance the student's creativity. This leads to sharing and healing of self and the integration of these dimensions in all aspects of one's being. This class experience builds trust in self as well as shows how to create a healing community with colleagues.

INTEGRATION OF HEALING RITUALS

We encourage the integration of rituals and the creative arts in each class as a way of connecting with the sacred life force. Rituals allow for uninterrupted attention of being present in the moment that allows natural healing to flow.

They are essential strategies for professional and personal integration of holistic principles. When students are exposed to rituals and the creative arts that evoke presence and healing, this unique quality time, in class as well as out of class requirements, will empower them to transfer this experience to clinical practice and other areas of their life. It will also assist them in future work situations to care for self and to support colleagues in their healing.

The rituals may be as simple as an opening guided relaxation and imagery exercise (10–15 minutes) incorporating music, or you may choose a longer experiential session using clay, mask-making, or drawing mandalas. An important aspect of inner work in our fast-paced lives is to create a time for rituals that have specific meaning. In creating a healing ritual (see Chapter 3), there are no absolute rules that should be followed. A ritual should have a structure—a beginning, a middle, and an end.

There are three phases to any ritual. To begin the first phase of a ritual—the *separation phase*—it is a symbolic act of breaking away from life's busy activities. In the second phase of ritual, the *transition phase*, we must create time to identify areas in our lives that need attention. The last phase of ritual, the *return phase*, is the reentry into daily life.

INSTRUCTOR'S ROLE

The instructor must be committed to health promotion, holistic principles, a healed state, and a formal releasing or putting aside the events of a crisis, and be experienced with and use complementary therapies in clinical practice and personal life. Develop your role as facilitator and coach in the integration of complementary healing modalities with traditional modalities in the classroom, clinical settings, and daily living. Encourage the students to focus on self-care as an important dimension of holistic nursing. Be creative in classroom presentation, discussion, and experiential activities.

Style. Use different teaching techniques and complementary modalities that allow your passion for caring and healing to emerge. Use your creative gifts. Which arts speak to you? How do you respond to music, art, paintings, weaving, sculpting, etc.? Remember one of your richest resources—your imagination!

Coaching Students. To assist students in the understanding and integration of the content, coach students in how to teach the experiential sessions on chosen class presentation. Students will present their ideas to the instructor. The instructor will coach students in how to guide classmates in different experiential exercises on chosen topics.

Guest Speakers. We encourage you to invite different speakers from the community who can bring relevance to different topics as well as to the inte-

6

gration of different healing modalities. Ask these experts to incorporate the use of the healing arts in their presentations if appropriate. Provide theory, clinical, and personal objectives from the specific textbook chapter if the topic is to be presented by a guest lecturer.

Audiovisual Aids. Incorporate slides, overheads, videos, and music to enhance the material. Arrange for a screen, pointer, audio cassette recorder or compact disc for playing music, and VCR and television for showing videos. Even if you are in a small classroom, the use of a microphone is encouraged.This assists the person leading the guided relaxation and imagery exercises to speak in a relaxed manner and not to strain his or her voice over background music. This also enhances the learning process of students in how to effectively use their voices as a therapeutic instrument of healing.

Healing Environment. Be creative with your classroom. Invite students to bring sitting floor pillows for experiential exercises. Hang colorful posters, display flowers and plants, and consider running water that flows into a small open reservoir vase or container (a small, inexpensive pump and container can be found at a garden nursery). You may even have some of your classes out in nature for sharing circles, walking meditation, etc. Encourage students to be tuned into the natural rhythms and cycles of nature. Use these naturally occurring events in nature as metaphors (the changing of the seasons, planting seeds, flowering, going into hibernation, etc.) in teaching situations and in the sharing of personal stories in healing circles.

Supplies for Healing Rituals. Some objects and supplies that can become ritual tools are: candles, music, drums, fabrics, altar or sacred space, circle, masks, songs, incense, healing symbols, totems, fetishes, poetry, chants, feathers, colored yarns, crayons, colored construction paper, pictures, stories, talking stick, flowers, water, earth elements, clay, and art supplies. Gather these art supplies and various healing objects as seen in Figures 1 and 2. Place supplies in baskets to be easily transported to class as well as a place to be stored between classes.

Healing Tapestry. This is a unique process experience and helps students to more quickly understand the qualities of recognizing and facilitating healing in self and others. You may wish to have students create a healing tapestry and add different qualities of healing in each class throughout the course. This tapestry can also be adapted to use with another topic discussed in the course. The steps for creating a healing tapestry are found in Appendix A and are seen in Figures 3 and 4. An adaptation to the healing tapestry exercise is seen in Figure 5. A guided imagery script that incorporate qualities of healing is presented in Appendix B.

Sharing Circles. Have students read Chapter 3, Nurse as Healer, in preparation for the second class session. This chapter focuses on essential

7

Figure 1 Art Supplies for Healing Rituals

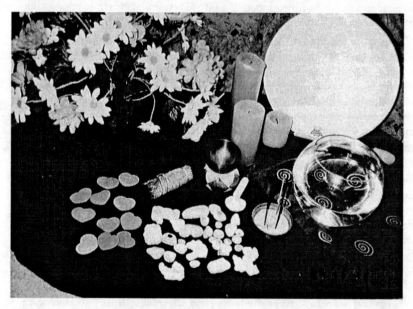

Figure 2 Objects for Healing Rituals

Figure 3 Blank Tapestry

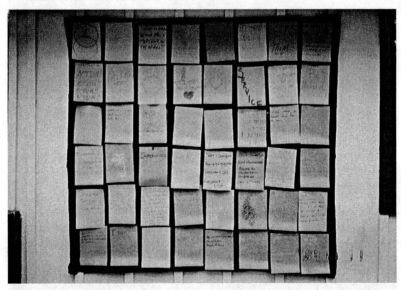

Figure 4 Healing Tapestry. Students have written healing qualities and drawn healing images and symbols on different pieces of colored construction paper. These are attached to the blank felt tapestry by placing the adhesive-backed male velcro dots to the back of the paper which easily adheres to an open square on the felt tapestry (see Appendix A for details).

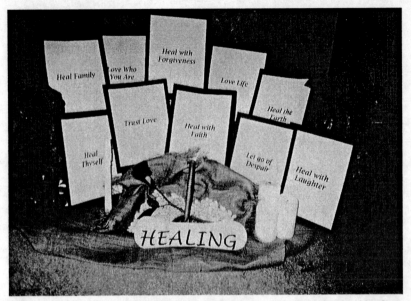

Figure 5 Recognizing Healing Qualities. Students have combined art and healing objects as part of a class presentation.

steps in healing, presence, the art of guiding, and real versus pseudo-listening. It prepares students for introduction to sharing circles. Sharing circles will be 15–20 minutes or longer in groups of 3–6 each class session. These sharing circles provides opportunities to exchange healing moments and any personal aspects that are in need of healing. This is to encourage the "listening council process."

Ask students to be mindful of the dialogue process and active listening. Encourage students to speak "from their heart." When the skills of speaking with intention are developed, an individual is able to be present and avoid superficial comments. To encourage reflection, suggest that students have a moment of silence before sharing. This is not a time for "psychoanalyzing" each other, but a time to practice presence in the moment and speaking from a place of authentic sharing. This helps in keeping the dialogue "open" because students learn to build trust and concern for self and others.

A talking stick or healing object may be used by a person before talking. Before speaking, a person will pick up a talking stick or a healing object and speak with intention. Only the person with the talking stick or healing object in their hand speaks. As students learn to be present with self, to hear stories of healing, joy, or deep pain, and to share the struggles and triumphs of one's own journey, they learn to validate the importance of caring and healing moments.

STUDENT'S ROLE

Class Session Topic(s). Read chapter(s) and complete homework assignment before each class. Come to class with an openness to develop new skills, to actively participate, and to increase understanding of what is meant by "allowing healing presence into each moment."

Annotated Bibliography Cards. Use chapter sections entitled Directions for Future Research as guidelines for literature review and weekly annotated bibliography cards.

Class Presentation. Active participation is essential. Students will choose a group and a topic and present a two-hour class presentation. This group will develop, plan, and prepare a handout and case study along with an experiential session related to the topic. This session will also require a practice and rehearsal outside of class. If a guest speaker is to be part of this class presentation, the students will work with the instructor to invite the best qualified person to present.

Attend 2 Different Group Support Meetings. Write a 3- to 5-page report on each meeting that reflects integration of health belief models, stages of change theory, holistic theory/strategies, and personal experiences.

Complete Circle of Human Potential Self-Assessments. Complete these self-assessments (Chapter 9) at the beginning and end of the course.

Mindfulness Practice. Students will begin a practice of mindfulness (10 minutes each day). This may include such strategies as relaxation, imagery, music, prayer, meditation, or movement such as a walking meditation. Suggestions for daily practice sessions may begin with "The part of me that is most in need of healing is" or "The parts of my life that I want to develop or to grow in are." See Appendix C for student guidelines.

Journaling. Begin journaling process (5 minutes each day). Encourage students to use Nurse Healer Reflections at the end of the assigned chapter(s) as a guide to journal entries. Students may also incorporate insights, emotions, changes in stress level, attitudes, healthier behaviors, or any difficulties in daily practice, etc. See Appendix D for student guidelines.

CHAPTER PREPARATION AND PRESENTATION

We recommend a four-stage process:

Process Exercise/Vision of Healing. Read the Process Exercise entitled Vision of Healing preceding each chapter for class discussion. What rings as truth when you read? Highlight these areas. Connect the Process Exercise with the Vision of Healing content. If one or more chapters are to be represented in the same class session, integrate the different process exercises throughout the class. Use guidelines given or develop a new ritual. Begin each class with an experiential exercise or a ritual that sets the stage and tone to evoke healing and presence. It will also help students gain a deeper understanding about how to create sacred space within one's self and be present in the moment.

Chapter Objectives. Be creative in how these are met. The theory objectives can be met by instructor presentation, guest lecturer, use of videos, experiential sessions, and weekly annotated bibliography cards. The clinical area objectives can be met in or out of the classroom in different community support group sessions, student group presentations, and experiential sessions. The personal objectives can be met by class participation, mindfulness practice, and journaling.

Quick Chapter Read-Through. Get an overall feel for chapter definitions and the content. Identify major themes you wish to present and highlight these areas.

Class Session Preparation. Allow 1 hour for structured presentation and 2 hours for experiential and sharing circles. Be flexible with these times depending on topic, use of guest speakers, videos, and student group presentation. Coach students on the most effective way to present the topic and experiential session.

CLOSING COURSE RITUAL

This process course will seem incomplete without a closing ritual. Invite a group of students to join you in creating a special closing celebration and a healing ritual. This may include the sharing of food and beverage. As the course evolves over the semester, you and the students will know exactly how to bring closure to the course.

AFTERWORD

We hope that this Instructor's Manual will help you and your students derive a rewarding experience from the textbook. If you would like to share your suggestions and creative endeavors with course curriculum and healing rituals for future editions of this instructor's manual and textbook, we would enjoy hearing from you.* We support and applaud you for creating this learning opportunity for students. Best wishes in your healing journey, work, and life.

Barbara Montgomery Dossey
Lynn Keegan
Cathie E. Guzzetta
Leslie Gooding Kolkmeier

---

*Send suggestions, course descriptions, and healing rituals to: Barbara Montgomery Dossey, RN, MS, FAAN, Director, Holistic Nursing Consultants, 878 Paseo Del Sur, Santa Fe, NM 87501.

Sample Course Description

COURSE TITLE

HOLISTIC NURSING: THE ART AND SCIENCE OF CARING AND HEALING

COURSE CREDIT

3 Credits

HOURS

45 theory and experiential hours

CURRICULUM PLACEMENT

Elective

PRE/CORE-REQUISITES

Senior Course Elective
Graduate Course Elective

CATALOGUE DESCRIPTION

Seminar discussion of holistic practice and interventions, demonstration and/or experiential sessions to facilitate an understanding of a holistic perspective in nursing practice and daily living. This course is specifically designed to assist students to comprehend the meaning of a holistic perspective for theory development, practice implications, and daily life.

CONCEPTUAL FRAMEWORK

The course is built on the dimensions that comprise the practice of holistic nursing: bio-psycho-social-spiritual theory, interventions, and research; nurse-focused, client/patient-focused, and family/significant others-focused concepts of caring/healing and health promotion; experiential interventions/strategies to enhance effective communication with self and others.

COURSE OBJECTIVES

At the completion of this course the student will be able to:

- Discuss the holistic dimension as a world view from a professional and personal perspective.
- Understand the purpose of holistic principles from a bio-psycho-social-spiritual perspective.
- Analyze how the holistic perspective is congruent with nursing's humanistic base.
- Evaluate various approaches of holistic modalities to clinical practice and daily life.
- Discuss how holistically oriented research findings can be implemented into clinical practice and daily life.
- Develop the ability to write and share theory and experiences from a holistic perspective.

OUTLINE

Holistic Nursing Practice, Dynamics of Consciousness and the Transpersonal Self, Nurse As Healer, Psychophysiology of Bodymind Healing, Exploring the Process of Change, Holistic Ethics, Holistic Approach to the Nursing Process, Nursing Research and Its Applications, Self-Assessments, Cognitive Therapy, Nutrition, Exercise, and Movement, Environment, Play and Laughter, Self-Reflection, Relationships, Sexual Abuse, Peaceful Deathing and Death, Weight Management, Smoking Cessation, Overcoming Addictions, Touch, Relaxation, Imagery, and Music Therapy.

TEACHING AND LEARNING STRATEGIES

- Seminar (theory, experiential sessions, slides, overheads, videos, handouts).
- In class: group presentation and class participation
- Out of class: 2 support group meetings of choice (12-Step programs, I Can Cope, HIV/AIDS, weight management, etc.); self-assessments; mindfulness practice (10 minutes a day); and journaling (5 minutes a day).
- Guest speakers (e.g., practitioners of Therapeutic Touch, biofeedback, art, music, movement, and/or healers from different cultures).

14

EVALUATION METHODS

20% Weekly annotated bibliography cards on 2 current journal articles related to class topic (1 research article and 1 article on related area of interest).

30% Group presentation that includes case study, handout, and experiential session that integrates holistic interventions.

20% Attend 2 different group support meetings. Write a 3- to 5-page report on each meeting that reflects integration of health belief model, stages of change theory, holistic theory/ strategies and personal experiences.

10% Complete Circle of Human Potential Self-Assessments at beginning and end of course.

20% Mindfulness Practice (10 minutes a day); Journaling (5 minutes each day).

REQUIRED TEXT

Dossey, B.M., Keegan, L., Guzzetta, C.E., and Kolkmeier, L.G. **Holistic Nursing: A Handbook for Practice,** 2nd ed. (Gaithersburg, MD: Aspen Publishers, Inc., 1995).

Sample Course Outline

Session 1

Course Introduction and Course Overview (1 hour).
Discuss that this is a process course and thus requires active participation. Stress importance of reading class assignment before coming to class. Give course requirements and guidelines for mindfulness practice and for journaling. Discuss the importance of mindfulness practice and self-reflection with journaling strategies for learning skills of being present in the moment. Student presentations begin with Session 5. Sessions 5–13 will be student presentations.
Introduce students to the five units of the textbook.

Unit I— Foundations for Healing and Holism
Unit II— Theory and Practice of Holistic Nursing
Unit III— Maximizing Human Potential
Unit IV— Lifestyle Alteration
Unit V— Holistic Nursing Interventions

Process Exercise #9
Chapter 9.   Self-Assessments: Facilitating Healing in Self and Others
              Complete Self-Assessments (Chapter 9) in class
              Review AHNA Standards of Holistic Nursing Practice (Chapter 1)

Session 2

Process Exercises #1, #2, and #4
Chapter 1.   Holistic Nursing Practice
Chapter 2.   Dynamics of Consciousness and the Transpersonal Self
Chapter 4.   The Psychophysiology of Bodymind Healing

Session 3

Process Exercises #3 and #14
Chapter 3.   Nurse As Healer
Chapter 14. Self-Reflection: Consulting the Truth Within
Appendix A: Guidelines for Creating a Healing Tapestry
Appendix B: Script: Creating a Healing Tapestry

Session 4

Process Exercises #6, #7, and #8
Chapter 6.   Holistic Ethics
Chapter 7.   Holistic Approach to the Nursing Process
Chapter 8.   Nursing Research and Holistic Implications

STUDENT PRESENTATIONS BEGIN WITH SESSION #5

Session 5

Process Exercises #5 and #10
Chapter 5.   Exploring the Process of Change
Chapter 10. Cognitive Therapy

Session 6

Process Exercise #22
Chapter 22. Relaxation: Opening the Door to Change

Session 7

Process Exercise #24
Chapter 24. Music Therapy : Hearing the Melody of the Soul

Session 8

Process Exercise #23
Chapter 23. Imagery: Awakening the Inner Healer

Session 9

Process Exercise #21
Chapter 21. Touch: Connecting with the Healing Power

Session 10

Process Exercise #13
Chapter 13. Play and Laughter: Moving toward Harmony

Session 11

Process Exercise #17
Chapter 17. Peaceful Deathing and Death

Session 12

Process Exercises #19 and #20
Chapter 19. Smoking Cessation: Breathing Free
Chapter 20. Overcoming Addictions: Recovering through Life

Session 13

Process Exercises #11 and #18
Chapter 11.   Nutrition, Exercise, and Movement
Chapter 18.   Weight Management: Eating More, Weighing Less

Session 14

Process Exercises #15 and #16
Chapter 15.   Relationships: Learning the Patterns and Processes
Chapter 16.   Sexual Abuse: Healing the Wounds

Session 15

Process Exercise #12
Chapter 12.   Environment: Protecting Our Personal and Planetary Home
Closing Ritual and Celebration

Information for Continuing Education

The American Holistic Nurses' Association (AHNA) has awarded Continuing Education credit for this course or course segment(s) (see Options I, II, III, and IV).

Holistic Nursing can be taught as a course or course segment(s) outside a university setting. The course or course segment(s) (see Options I, II, III, and IV) must be taught and developed by a holistic nurse (minimum of a baccalaureate degree in nursing) and can be sponsored by the following:

- a holistic nurse who develops a course or course segment(s) on holistic nursing practice as part of an in independent practice
- a holistic nurse who develops a course or course segment(s) on holistic nursing practice for a hospital/medical center nursing education development and research department
- a holistic nurse who develops a course or course segment(s) on holistic nursing practice for a community continuing education program such as winter, spring, summer, or fall series.

Note: For information on other AHNA holistic nursing and healing touch courses contact:

American Holistic Nurses' Association
4101 Lake Boone Trail
Suite #201
Raleigh, North Carolina 27607
Phone (919) 787-5181
FAX (919) 787-4915

HOLISTIC NURSING COURSE/COURSE SEGMENT(S) DESCRIPTIONS

To obtain Continuing Education fee and Continuing Education certificate information, contact:

Bodymind Systems
910 Dakota Drive
Temple, Texas 76504
Phone (817) 773-2337
FAX (817) 773-3052

Course/Course Segment(s):	**Holistic Nursing.** Course/course segment(s) based on the textbook and Instructor's Manual for *Holistic Nursing: A Handbook for Practice*, 2nd ed, B.M. Dossey, L. Keegan, C.E. Guzzetta, & L.G. Kolkmeier (Gaithersburg, MD: Aspen Publishers, 1995).
Program:	**Holistic Nursing Option I.** (See Instructor's Manual) All 15 sessions (3 hours each)
Contact Hours Awarded:	54.0 contact hours
Program:	**Holistic Nursing Option II.** (See Instructor's Manual) Any 6 topic combination of 3-hour course segment(s) (Example: Holistic Nursing, Nurse As Healer, Relaxation, Imagery, Music, and Touch)
Contact Hours Awarded:	21.6 Contact Hours
Program:	**Holistic Nursing Option III.** (See Instructor's Manual) Any topic combination of 3-hour course segment(s) (Example: Relaxation and Imagery)
Contact Hours Awarded:	7.2 Contact Hours
Program:	**Holistic Nursing Option IV.** (See Instructor's Manual) Any 3-hour course segment (Example: Imagery)
Contact Hours Awarded:	3.6 Contact Hours

FOUNDATIONS FOR HEALING AND HOLISM

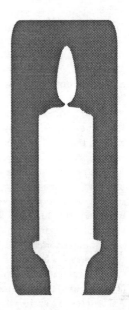

Chapter 1

Holistic Nursing Practice

CHAPTER OBJECTIVES

Refer to chapter for specific theory, clinical, and personal objectives. These will provide guidelines for the integration of objectives in class presentation, experiential sessions, and student homework assignments.

CHAPTER OVERVIEW

Two major challenges have emerged in nursing. The first challenge is to integrate the concepts of technology, mind, and spirit into nursing practice. The second challenge is to create models for health care that guide the healing of self and others. Holistic nursing is the most complete way to conceptualize and practice professional nursing.

PROCESS EXERCISE # 1

(15-minute opening experiential session using music and healing objects if desired)

Vision of Healing: Exploring Life's Meaning

As we explore meaning and purpose, we are able to access those events that are most important as well as to more easily identify passions in life. Meanings are individual and personal. As we explore our personal experience with daily events, we move closer to a deeper understanding of holism.

Begin with a guided relaxation exercise (5 minutes) and gradually fade in music of choice. Suggest to students that they can close their eyes or leave their eyes open. If eyes are left open ask them to find a spot several feet in front of them to focus on. This allows for a greater ease in following the relaxation and imagery suggestions and reflective experience.

Using techniques for empowering relaxation and imagery scripts (see pp. 619–622), gently weave into a guided imagery exercise reflective questions from the Spiritual Assessment Tool (Exhibit 1–1) such as, "What gives your life meaning and purpose? What are your inner strengths? When you feel a deep sense of interconnection with yourself, with others, or with the universe, what is your experience?" Add three to five more reflective questions under each of the categories (set in boldface type). Bring closure to the imagery process.

With soft music still playing, invite students to record in a personal journal (3–5 minutes) any images, process questions and answers, or insight gained. Ask students to bring personal closure to this process. Gradually fade music out. Engage students in a gentle stretching exercise before the theory session begins.

KEY CONCEPTS: THEORY

(1-hour presentation)
OPTIONAL: GUEST SPEAKER(S) AND VIDEO(S)

Guest Speaker(s): Invite a nurse who integrates holistic modalities in clinical practice or a panel of nurses in different practice settings that are guided in practice by a bio-psycho-social-spiritual model. Provide guest speaker(s) with the Instructor's Manual suggestions to become familiar with students' assignment before class.

Video(s): Show a video of a practitioner describing and demonstrating one or more holistic modalities (rent from media catalog or purchase for school video library). Following the video presentation ask students for their reaction and comments. Discuss video and answer questions.

Definitions: Review definitions and incorporate into presentation.

Holistic Nursing: Review natural systems theory (Figure 1–1). Explain the Western, allopathic medical model (Table 1–1) that has been used for the last 150 years in diagnoses and treatment of disease. Discuss how this model is incomplete as the remaining topics in this section are integrated.

Mind/Body Dilemma: Contrast the allopathic and holistic models of care. Discuss the Office of Alternative Medicine (OAM) at the National Institutes of Health. Integrate the OAM mission statement and research opportunities.

Eras of Medicine: Review the dynamics of the Eras of Medicine framework (Figure 1–2 and Table 1–2). Focus on states of consciousness and therapies in each— local states of consciousness in Eras I and II, and nonlocal states of consciousness in Era III.

"Doing" and "Being" Therapies: Discuss the "doing" and "not-doing" approaches (Figure 1–3) to healing.

Rational and Paradoxical Healing: Discuss concepts and therapies of rational and paradoxical healing (Figure 1–4). Develop the linear and nonlinear dynamics of healing.

Bio-Psycho-Social-Spiritual Model: Contrast the bio-psycho-social and the bio-psycho-social-spiritual model (Figure 1–5). Discuss the interdependence and the interrelatedness of all parts. Review the Joint Commission Patient Bill of Rights.

Distinguishing Spiritual Elements and Psychologic Elements: Discuss the differences in spiritual and psychologic elements.

EXPERIENTIAL EXERCISES

(2 hours. Incorporation of sharing circles (see pp. 7 and 10) and experiential exercises is encouraged for class presentation.)

Description of Holistic Nursing and the Standards for Holistic Nursing Practice: Provide an overview of the American Holistic Nurses' Association (AHNA) Working Description of Holistic Nursing and the AHNA Standards of Holistic Nursing Practice (see Appendix 1–A).

Have students work in 14 small groups. Each group will explore one part of the AHNA Standards in depth. The Nurse-Focused Concepts section has 2 parts and the Client/Patient-Focused Concepts section has 12 parts. Allow time for each group to present comments/ideas from their assigned part of the AHNA Standards.

Ask students to share insight gained since Session 1 about increased awareness or importance of recognizing self-care concepts and the Circle of Human Potential (Chapter 9) each day.

Rational and Paradoxical Healing and "Doing" and "Being" Therapies: Present a case study that incorporates rational/paradoxical and doing/being therapies. Have students share any personal stories or situations where holistic modalities have been integrated, declined by client/pa-

23

tient/family, or either allopathic physicians or nurses have blocked the use of holistic modalities in the clinical setting.

Characteristics of Spirituality: Have students work in dyads and take turns asking questions from the Spiritual Assessment Tool (Exhibit 1–1) categories of *meaning* and *purpose, inner strengths,* and *interconnections.* Assess those questions that are easy to answer and those that are difficult.

Invite students to share with the group the insight and experiences with evoking personal information in these three areas. Have students explore the differences in intellectually answering these questions as compared to being guided in an imagery exercise with these questions in the Process Exercise #1 at the beginning of class. Repeat a guided imagery exercise using the questions from the Spiritual Assessment Tool.

ANNOTATED BIBLIOGRAPHY CARDS

Directions for Future Research: Have students choose one or more research questions as an area to explore for annotated bibliography cards. Encourage students to begin collecting articles that can support further investigation.

JOURNAL ENTRIES

Nurse Healer Reflections: Encourage students to use the chapter reflective questions as a guide to journal entries for exploring, understanding, and validating presence and healing.

Chapter 2

Dynamics of Healing and the Transpersonal Self

CHAPTER OBJECTIVES

Refer to chapter for specific theory, clinical, and personal objectives. These will provide guidelines for the integration of objectives in class presentation, experiential sessions, and student homework assignments.

CHAPTER OVERVIEW

Over the last 25 years, health care has been based on the allopathic, masculine model that has focused on the curing of symptoms. Individuals now recognize that both the allopathic approaches combined and integrated with complementary healing modalities are needed to stabilize or reverse disease and to improve their quality of life.

PROCESS EXERCISE #2

(15-minute opening experiential session using music and healing objects if desired)

Vision of Healing: The Transpersonal Self

An important part of holistic nursing is connecting with inner healing resources. When nurses strive to explore their healing resources as a first step on the journey toward wholeness, they acknowledge inner wisdom essential to the healing process.

Begin with a guided relaxation exercise (5 minutes) and gradually fade in music of choice. Suggest to students that they can close their eyes or leave their eyes open. If eyes are open ask them to find a spot several feet in front of them to focus on. This allows for a greater ease in following the relaxation and imagery suggestions and reflective experience.

Using techniques for empowering relaxation and imagery scripts (see pp. 619–622), gently weave into a guided imagery exercise reflective questions about masculine and feminine qualities (Table 2–1). Incorporate the importance of honoring both ways of being into clinical practice and personal life. Bring closure to the imagery process.

With soft music still playing, invite students to record in a personal journal (3–5 minutes) any images, process questions and answers, or insight gained. Ask students to bring personal closure to this process. Gradually fade music out. Engage students in a gentle stretching exercise before the theory session begins.

KEY CONCEPTS: THEORY

(1-hour presentation)
OPTIONAL: GUEST SPEAKER(S) AND VIDEO(S)

Guest Speaker(s): Invite one or more nurses who have envisioned partnerships in clinical practice and have transformed parts of an established hospital system. Provide guest speaker(s) with the Instructor's Manual suggestions to become familiar with students' assignment before class.

Video(s): Show a video of a nurse or a group of nurses describing and demonstrating the integration of holistic modalities and change in a traditional health care setting (rent from media catalog or purchase for school video library). Following the video presentation ask students for their reaction and comments. Discuss video and answer questions.

Definitions: Review definitions and incorporate into presentation.

The Healing System: Discuss the difference in curing and healing. Explore the interconnections of all parts of a healing system (Figure 2–1).

A Human Science: Discuss the concepts of Watson's model of human caring (Figure 2–2).

Transpersonal Human Care and Caring Transactions: Develop the five major themes identified in caring/healing research; review authenticity and healing awareness.

Path toward Transpersonal Healing: Discuss the complex factors that shape and influence the nurse's and client's/patient's world view.

Physical Health vs. Spiritual Health: Explore the problems and fallacies when physical and spiritual health are viewed as the same. Contrast the examples of unhealthy saints and mystics with healthy reprobates (Figure 2–3).

EXPERIENTIAL EXERCISES

(2 hours. Incorporation of sharing circles (see pp. 7 and 10) and experiential exercises is encouraged for class presentation.)

Integration of Personal and Professional Mission Statements: Review several prototype health care systems that have integrated a holistic model. Ask students to write and integrate their personal and professional mission statements.

Envisioning Partnerships: Explore attributes of successful partnerships listed under effective partnering (Exhibit 2–1). Ask students to share what it feels like to go beyond "I" strategies to "we" strategies. Have each student identify their leadership skills and how these can be incorporated to build effective partnerships in their current clinical situations or other activities such as personal life, organizations, community work, etc. Allow time for group discussion.

ANNOTATED BIBLIOGRAPHY CARDS

Directions for Future Research: Have students choose one or more research questions as an area to explore for annotated bibliography cards. Encourage students to begin collecting articles that can support further investigation.

JOURNAL ENTRIES

Nurse Healer Reflections: Encourage students to use the chapter reflective questions as a guide to journal entries for exploring, understanding, and validating presence and healing.

Chapter 3

Nurse As Healer

CHAPTER OBJECTIVES

Refer to chapter for specific theory, clinical, and personal objectives. These will provide guidelines for the integration of objectives in class presentation, experiential sessions, and student homework assignments.

CHAPTER OVERVIEW

Being a nurse healer allows the nurse an opportunity to explore the inner dimensions of personal, interpersonal, and transpersonal growth. Awareness of healing and healer allows a presence where nurse–client/patient interactions take on new dimensions.

PROCESS EXERCISE #3

(15-minute opening experiential session using music and healing objects if desired)

Vision of Healing: Toward the Inward Journey

True nurse healing requires attention to one's strengths and weaknesses and to purpose and the meaning in life. As the parts of self that are in need of healing are discovered, the nurse is able to be more fully present in the moment to assist others with their healing.

Begin with a guided relaxation exercise (5 minutes) and gradually fade in soft music of choice. Suggest to students that they can close their eyes or leave their eyes open. If eyes are left open, ask students to find a spot several feet in front of them to focus on. This allows for a greater ease in following the relaxation and imagery suggestions and reflective experience.

Using techniques for empowering relaxation and imagery scripts (see text, pp. 619–622), gently weave into a guided imagery exercise reflective questions created from the characteristics/qualities of a nurse healer (pp. 63–64). Suggest to students to resonant with each characteristic/quality and to notice which have a ring of truth and those characteristics/ qualities that need to be developed. Bring closure to the imagery process.

With soft music still playing, invite students to record in a personal journal (3–5 minutes) any images, process questions and answers, or insight gained. Ask students to bring personal closure to this process. Gradually fade music out. Engage students in a gentle stretching exercise before the theory session begins.

KEY CONCEPTS: THEORY

(1 hour presentation)
OPTIONAL: GUEST SPEAKER(S) AND VIDEO(S)

Guest Speaker(s): Invite one or more nurses who are exploring the concept of presence and healing in clinical practice. Provide guest speaker(s) with the Instructor's Manual suggestions to become familiar with students' assignment before class.

Video(s): Show a video of a nurse describing and demonstrating presence and healing in clinical practice (rent from media catalog or purchase for school video library). Following the video presentation ask students for their reaction and comments. Discuss video and answer questions.

Definitions: Review definitions and incorporate into presentation.

Patterns of Knowing and Unknowing: Discuss the four recognized patterns of knowing— empirical knowledge, personal knowledge, ethical knowledge, and aesthetic knowledge as well as the pattern of unknowing. Explore the characteristic of a nurse-healer.

Purpose: Discuss the dimensions and characteristic of individual growth (Figure 3–1 and Table 3–1). Explore how development of these dimensions can assist individuals to identify a sense of meaning and purpose in life's journey.

The Art of Guiding: Explain the developmental process of the art of guiding and that it requires skills of presence. These skills can be developed in many ways such as mindfulness practice, relaxation, imagery, music, and so forth.

Myth of Chiron: Review the myth of Chiron. Discuss how this myth is a way of addressing the harmony as well as the imbalance that always occurs throughout life.

Presence: Discuss three levels of presence—physical, psychological, and therapeutic presence and the healing qualities/states in each level (Table 3–2).

Working with Others: Discuss the healing outcomes when we work and live our lives from a holistic perspective.

Rituals of Healing: Explore the three phases of rituals— separation, transition, and return. Discuss the ritual guide to getting well (Exhibit 3–1).

EXPERIENTIAL EXERCISES

(2 hours. Incorporation of sharing circles (see pp. 7 and 10) and experiential exercises is encouraged for class presentation.)

Affirmation of Exceptional Qualities: Have students work in dyads and share with each other the inner experience when the affirmations of exceptional qualities are used. Explore the exceptional qualities/statements that feel correct and those that are hard to identify. Ask students to assess how often affirmations of exceptional qualities are used throughout the day.

Real vs. Pseudo-Listening: Explore the three components of any communication process and the signs of pseudo-listening. Have students work in dyads and take turns first in a pseudo-listening experience followed by a listening experience with intention. Share the experience.

Laughter, Humor, and Joy: Explore how joy and sadness pathways cannot operate simultaneously. Develop how these events serve as a mini-relaxation strategy and as a healing and therapeutic intervention.

Sharing Our Healing Stories: Examine the terms *dialogue* and *healthy dialogue*. Explore the body-mind-spirit process and effects of trust and fear levels. Have students share different situations where they can remember operating out of fear rather than from a level of trust (Table 3–3). Explore themes, concepts, and practice characteristics of expert nurses (Table 3–4).

ANNOTATED BIBLIOGRAPHY CARDS

Directions for Future Research: Have students choose one or more research questions as an area to explore for annotated bibliography cards. Encourage students to begin collecting articles that can support further investigation.

JOURNAL ENTRIES

Nurse Healer Reflections: Encourage students to use chapter reflective questions as a guide to journal entries for exploring, understanding, and validating presence and healing.

UNIT II

THEORY AND PRACTICE OF HOLISTIC NURSING

Chapter 4

The Psychophysiology of Bodymind Healing

CHAPTER OBJECTIVES

Refer to chapter for specific theory, clinical, and personal objectives. These will provide guidelines for the integration of objectives in class presentation, experiential sessions, and student homework assignments.

CHAPTER OVERVIEW

Information theory, transduction, self-regulation theory, and mind modulation of the autonomic, endocrine, immune, and neuropeptide systems serve as a theoretical basis for bodymind healing. Nurses can reduce the devastating effects of illness of clients/patients and their families when they address the bio-psycho-social-spiritual human dimensions and integrate holistic nursing interventions in clinical practice.

PROCESS EXERCISE #4

(15-minute opening experiential session using music and healing objects if desired)

Vision of Healing: The Evolving Dance of Life

Healing ourselves and facilitating healing in others requires that we acknowledge the parts of our lives that are in need of healing. The following exercise is an excellent example of state-dependent learning and memory. It demonstrates how to access a hurt from the past and how to create a reframe of healing the hurt.

Share with students that the first part of this exercise is to remember a part of self that is in need of healing. The second part of the exercise is to create the healing. This may bring tears or different emotions may surface. If any students are uncomfortable with a memory that has been accessed, they can stay with the image and see what follows, or tell them to take a deep breath, open their eyes, and the images at that discomfort level will leave. There is no right or wrong. If they choose not to participate at a depth level, suggest that they can intellectually go through the exercise and be exposed to a tool for facilitating deep healing.

Begin with a guided relaxation exercise (5 minutes) and gradually fade in soft music of choice. Suggest to students that they can close their eyes or leave their eyes open. If eyes are left open, ask students to find a spot several feet in front of them to focus on. This allows for a greater ease in following the relaxation and imagery suggestions and reflective experience.

Using techniques for empowering relaxation and imagery scripts (see pp. 619-622), gently weave into a guided imagery exercise the following reflective questions. Let yourself go back in time between the ages of five and ten. If it seems right, allow a painful memory, a disappointment, or a failure to come into conscious awareness and any details that may be remembered. Use all of your senses. Just be present and experience what comes into your awareness. It might be a time of remembering being embarrassed, feeling ashamed, or being physically or emotionally hurt. How old are you? What are you wearing? Where are you? Who is there with you? This may bring tears or different emotions may surface. Stay with this experience for a while.

Let yourself now in your wise grown voice tell this little person that he or she is okay. With your lovingkindness, your compassion, tell this child comforting words that can bring about some healing of this experience. Hug or kiss the child. Just listen to the words, images, or feelings that come. You will know actually what needs to be healed at this time. Tell the child within that you are always there and that you are always available to listen to past memories that are in need of healing. Next tell yourself that you are okay. Give yourself some thoughts about this part of yourself that is still in need of healing. Bring closure to the imagery process.

31

With soft music still playing, invite students to record in a personal journal (3–5 minutes) any images, process questions and answers, or insight gained. Encourage students to use journaling or other modalities to continue to evoke deep healing. Ask students to bring personal closure to this process. Gradually fade music out. Engage students in a gentle stretching exercise before the theory session begins.

KEY CONCEPTS: THEORY

(1-hour presentation)
OPTIONAL: GUEST SPEAKER(S) AND VIDEO(S)

Guest Speaker(s): Invite one or more nurses who use hypnotherapy in clinical practice to present the theory and to demonstrate different strategies to access state-dependent learning and memory. Provide guest speaker(s) with the Instructor's Manual suggestion to become familiar with students' assignment before class.

Video(s): Show a video that explores bodymind theories and modalities (rent from media catalog or purchase for school video library). Following the video presentation ask students for their reaction and comments. Discuss video and answer questions.

Definitions: Review definitions and incorporate into presentation.

Information Theory: Discuss how information theory is a mathematical model that emerged with modern communication technologies. Explain how information theory is a model capable of unifying physiologic, psychologic, sociologic, and spiritual phenomena and explaining the connections of consciousness and bodymind healing.

Transduction: Explore the nature of transduction as the conversion of energy or information from one form to another. Discuss the different research studies and the holistic interventions that demonstrate information transduction.

State-Dependent Learning and Memory: Explore how state-dependent learning and memory influences how we perform and what we remember. Discuss the four integrated hypotheses about memory and learning. Connect this discussion with the opening process exercise.

Location of Brain Centers: Discuss the conflicts between the traditional neuroanatomic model, information theory, and mind modulation.

Self-Regulation Theory: Explore cybernetic feedback loops and cognitive, emotional, spiritual, and biochemical responses with images and information.

Mind Modulation of the Autonomic Nervous System: Explore the three stages of mind modulation of the autonomic nervous system. Discuss the healing outcomes to various body parts and body cells with holistic modalities (Figure 4–2).

Mind Modulation of the Endocrine System: Discuss the central tenet of neuroendocrinology—neurosecretion and its relationship to learning, memory, pain, perception, addictions, appetite, etc. (Figure 4–3). Examine hormones that have been identified as having bodymind function (Exhibit 4–1).

The Mind Gene Connection: Explore the three stages of mind-gene process.

Mind Modulation of the Immune System: Discuss psychoneuro-immunology and the bidirectional circuitry of these three systems (Figure 4–4). Examine the research discussed on the direct correlation between relaxation, imagery, immunology, and mind modulation of the immune system.

Mind Modulation of the Neuropeptide System: Discuss neuropeptides and their receptor sites and the bodymind interconnections and the ways in which people experience emotions in their body (Figure 4–5).

EXPERIENTIAL EXERCISES

(2 hours. Incorporation of sharing circles (see pp. 7 and 10) and experiential exercises is encouraged for class presentation.)

Ultradian Performance Rhythm: Examine ultradian rhythms, ultradian stress syndrome, and ultradian performance rhythms. Review the three major implications to consider in regard to the ultradian healing response (Figure 4–1). Ask students to plot out the current day and to see at what times they have applied ultradian theory and healing strategies in their personal lives—what kept them from taking breaks, eating a nutritious lunch, exercise, etc.

Have students integrate ultradian rhythms to one or more of their desired behavioral changes.

Encourage students to create a healing room for themselves at home. Ask students to explore with colleagues in the work environment ideas of ultradian breaks.

If there are communication difficulties with colleagues at work, integrate Process Exercise #15 (Chapter 15) on accepting ourselves and others.

Clinical Implications for the Future: Discuss the rapid changes in the knowledge base of psychoneuroimmunology. Explore nurses' challenges in clinical practice to refine the processes and techniques for specific modulation of bodymind symptoms.

ANNOTATED BIBLIOGRAPHY CARDS

Directions for Future Research: Have students choose one or more research questions as an area to explore for annotated bibliography cards. Encourage students to begin collecting articles that can support further investigation.

JOURNAL ENTRIES

Nurse Healer Reflections: Encourage students to use the chapter reflective questions as a guide to journal entries for exploring, understanding, and validating presence and healing.

Chapter 5

Exploring the Process of Change

CHAPTER OBJECTIVES

Refer to chapter for specific theory, clinical, and personal objectives. These will provide guidelines for the integration of objectives in class presentation, experiential sessions, and student homework assignments.

CHAPTER OVERVIEW

As nurses become more aware of the health-wellness-disease-illness continuum, they can more easily assist individuals in investigating the meaning of an acute crisis or illness. Values clarification, the Health Belief Model, and stages of change explain the complexities that people confront and why certain behaviors exist. These concepts and theories can increase the nurse's awareness of the way in which values and beliefs affect each element of the motivational process and stages of change. People must be motivated and engaged in the change process before they can begin to change behavior and to sustain maintenance behaviors that move them toward well-being.

PROCESS EXERCISE #5

(15-minute opening experiential session using music and other healing objects if desired)

Vision of Healing: Reawakening Spirit in Daily Life

When we exhibit hardiness characteristics we can maximize our human potentials. The three hardiness characteristics, referred to as the 3 Cs, are change, challenge, and control.

Begin with a guided relaxation exercise (5 minutes) and gradually fade in music of choice. Suggest to students that they can close their eyes or leave their eyes open. If eyes are open ask them to find a spot several feet in front of them to focus on. This allows for a greater ease in following the relaxation and imagery suggestions and reflective experience.

Using techniques for empowering relaxation and imagery scripts (pp. 619–622), gently weave into a guided imagery exercise reflective questions about the 3Cs. Next weave the seven reflective questions discussed under work spirit into the imagery process. Bring closure to the imagery process.

With soft music still playing, invite students to record in a personal journal (3–5 minutes) any images, process questions and answers, or insight gained. Ask students to bring personal closure to this process. Gradually fade music out. Engage students in a gentle stretching exercise before the theory session begins.

KEY CONCEPTS: THEORY

(1-hour presentation)
OPTIONAL: GUEST SPEAKER(S) AND VIDEO(S)

Guest Speaker(s): Invite one or more nurses who direct a corporate wellness center. Provide guest speaker(s) with the Instructor's Manual suggestions to become familiar with students' assignment before class.

Video(s): Show a video of practitioner(s) describing and demonstrating one or more folk medicine healing rituals (rent from media catalog or purchase for school video library). Following video presentation ask students for their reaction and comments. Discuss video and answer questions.

Definitions: Review definitions and incorporate into presentation.

Concepts of Health-Wellness-Disease-Illness: Explore the relationship between health, wellness, disease, and illness by reviewing the definition of each. Discuss the importance of exploring the dynamics of each concept such as the actual or perceived function/dysfunction through the interactions of cognitive-affective dimensions that are developed in text. Review knowledge of general patterns of responses for specific cultural and ethnic groups as a guideline for assessment and individualized care (Table 5–1).

Health Behaviors: Explore *engagement* and *lack of engagement* as more appropriate terms than *compliant* and *noncompliant* when people change or do not change health behaviors.

Worksite Wellness: Explore the steps to take in developing a wellness program. Review known circumstances that will block a person's motivated behavior.

EXPERIENTIAL EXERCISES

(2 hours. Incorporation of sharing circles (see pp. 7 and 10) and experiential exercises is encouraged for class presentation.)

Values Clarification: Explore the difference in attitudes, beliefs, and values. Review the values clarification process—choosing, prizing, and acting. Have students assess whether they have more attitudes and beliefs than they have values about exercise, relaxation, and play. For example, a student believes that exercise is important for health and that it also serves as a stress manager and assists with a sense of inner peace and harmony. However, this student has no exercise routine. Thus, this student has attitudes and beliefs about exercise but assigns it no value. Have students use the above example and create a set of values for exercise (or another behavior that is desired) by using the three steps in the values clarification process.

Health Belief Model: Explore the major factors in determining a person's engagement in choosing new health behaviors. Examine the relationship of health beliefs, attitudes, and social support to facilitate engagement . Review the four categories of the Health Belief Model.

Stages of Change: Review the 5 stages of change and the characteristics of each stage (Figure 5–1). Explore the dynamic of the change process and the most appropriate interventions in each stage (Tables 5–2 and 5–3).

ANNOTATED BIBLIOGRAPHY CARDS

Directions for Future Research: Have students choose one or more research questions as an area to explore for annotated bibliography cards. Encourage students to begin collecting articles that can support further investigation.

JOURNAL ENTRIES

Nurse Healer Reflections: Encourage students to use the chapter reflective questions as a guide to journal entries for exploring, understanding, and validating presence and healing.

Chapter 6

Holistic Ethics

CHAPTER OBJECTIVES

Refer to chapter for specific theory, clinical, and personal objectives. These will assist with the integration of objectives in class presentation, experiential sessions, and student homework assignments.

CHAPTER OVERVIEW

Holistic ethics provides the framework and guidelines for the development of a healing attitude and morality in healers. Ethics serves as a foundation to teach individuals specific strategies to release the self (ego) and to access the wisdom of the transpersonal dimension.

PROCESS EXERCISE #6

(15-minute opening experiential session using music and healing objects if desired)

Vision of Healing: Ethics in Our Changing World

As we explore our own moral values and behaviors, we are able to access events that help shape who we are and why we behave as we do. Then as we link our personal behaviors with our daily life experiences, we move closer to a deeper understanding of holism. As you guide students, ask them to reflect on the choices they make in different scenarios and to consider how their choices reflect their ethics.

Begin with a guided relaxation exercise (5 minutes) and gradually fade in music of choice. Suggest to students that they can close their eyes or leave their eyes open. If eyes are left open ask them to find a spot several feet in front of them to focus on. This allows for a greater ease in following the suggestions and reflective experience.

Using techniques for empowering relaxation and imagery scripts (see pp. 619–622), gently weave into a guided imagery exercise reflective questions as follows: What gives your life meaning and purpose? On what grounds do you base your routine decisions? Your major life decisions? With what actions do you feel a deep sense of interconnection with yourself, with others, or with the universe? Add three to five more reflective questions about ethics from a holistic perspective. Bring closure to the imagery process.

With soft music still playing, invite students to record in a personal journal (3–5 minutes) any images, process questions and answers, or insight gained. Ask students to bring personal closure to this process. Gradually fade music out. Engage students in a gentle stretching exercise before the theory session begins.

KEY CONCEPTS: THEORY

(1-hour presentation)
OPTIONAL: GUEST SPEAKERS(S) AND VIDEO(S)

Guest Speaker(s): Invite one or more nurses experienced in ethical issues. Provide guest speaker(s) with the Instructor's Manual suggestions to become familiar with the students' assignment before class.

Video(s): Show a video of an ethical issue (rent from local video store or media catalog or purchase for school video library). Following the video presentation ask students for their reaction and comments. Discuss video and answer questions.

Definitions: Review definitions and incorporate into presentation.

The Nature of Ethical Problems: Increase the students' awareness of the range and scope of ethical dilemmas. Introduce aspects of life-prolonging technology to illustrate the complexity of death and dying issues.

Morals and Principles: Discuss the three primary principles of biomedical ethics. Introduce the four conditions of the principle of double effect. Discuss the meaning of these four conditions and integrate clinical examples.

Traditional Ethical Theories: Review the basic theories on which Western ethics is based. Introduce and discuss the terms *deontologic* and *teleologic* and discuss the meaning of each term. Integrate the presuppositions of the new theory of holistic ethics. Discuss the Code of Ethics for Holistic Nurses (Exhibit 6-1).

Holistic Ethics and Consciousness: Discuss the concept and dimensions of consciousness. Explore the three levels of consciousness. Begin a discussion about how the levels of consciousness relates to the theory of holistic ethics.

Analysis of Ethical Dilemmas: Introduce the four-step concept of ethical analysis. Explore each of the four steps and relate each step to one or more clinical situations.

EXPERIENTIAL EXERCISES

(2 hours. Incorporation of sharing circles (see pp. 7 and 10) and experiential exercises is encouraged for class presentation. Refer to chapter section entitled Specific Interventions for details.)

Case Analysis: Present a case history/story, either from your own clinical experience or from the literature. Ask the students to refer to Jonsen's four-component analysis technique, and then analyze the case history/story. Depending on the time available and the number of students present you may include the following: small student group discussion, writing the four components on a board/poster/overhead and leading a class discussion of each component, or asking student group leaders to present their groups' analyses to the class.

Have students also discuss case studies from their personal life experiences. Encourage students to share other patient stories and to focus on the meaning of the symptoms, disease, illness, and use of specific symbols and metaphors.

Advance Medical Directives: Review the key points of the 1991 Patient Self-Determination Act. Discuss the assessment questions a nurse may consider asking during the intake interview.

Story Telling: Use the metaphor of storytelling to make points about ethical situations. Collect stories from the literature or share your own stories based on your clinical experiences.

ANNOTATED BIBLIOGRAPHY CARDS

Directions for Future Research: Have students choose one or more research questions as an area to explore for annotated bibliography cards. Encourage students to begin collecting articles that can support further investigation.

JOURNAL ENTRIES

Nurse Healer Reflections: Encourage students to use the chapter reflective questions as a guide to journal entries for exploring, understanding, and validating presence and healing.

Chapter 7

Holistic Approach to the Nursing Process

CHAPTER OBJECTIVES

Refer to chapter for specific theory, clinical, and personal objectives. These will assist with the integration of objectives in class presentation, experiential sessions, and student homework assignments.

CHAPTER OVERVIEW

The nursing process has been incorporated into academic and clinical settings to ensure quality nursing care to maintain the client's health, maximize the client's resources, or return the client to a state of health. The nursing process includes six steps: 1) client assessment, 2) nursing diagnosis, 3) client outcomes, 4) therapeutic care planning, 5) implementation of care, and 6) evaluation. The nursing process is an ongoing, orderly, systematic, and flexible set of actions to guide in the integration of holistic principles.

PROCESS EXERCISE #10

(15-minute opening experiential session using music and healing objects if desired)

Vision of Healing: Human Care

Human care involves a client-centered focused process of caring and healing. As nurses explore holistic principles and develop the skills of self-care and presence, human care is at the core of all actions.

Begin with a guided relaxation exercise (5 minutes) and gradually fade in music of choice. Suggest to students that they can close their eyes or leave their eyes open. If eyes are open ask them to find a spot several feet in front of them to focus on. This allows for a greater ease in following the relaxation and imagery suggestions and reflective experience.

Using techniques for empowering relaxation and imagery scripts (pp. 619–622), gently weave into a guided imagery exercise reflective questions using the nursing process framework. In the imagination, slowly guide students in assessing and diagnosing their own body-mind-spirit. Then ask them to create an outcome, plan, and intervention for achieving more balance and harmony in one area of their life. And finally ask them to imagine an evaluation process for the desired outcome. Bring closure to the imagery process.

With soft music still playing, invite students to record in a personal journal (3–5 minutes) any images, process questions and answers, or insight gained. Ask students to bring personal closure to this process. Gradually fade music out. Engage students in a gentle stretching exercise before the theory session begins.

KEY CONCEPTS: THEORY

(1-hour presentation)
OPTIONAL: GUEST SPEAKERS(S) AND VIDEO(S)

Guest Speakers(s): Invite one or more nurses to discuss the dynamics of developing, using, integrating, a holistic assessment tool in clinical practice. Provide guest speaker(s) with the Instructor's Manual suggestions to become familiar with students' assignment before class.

Video(s): Show a video of a practitioner who describes, demonstrates, and integrates holistic assessment tools and nursing process in clinical practice (rent from media catalog or purchase for school video library). Following the video presentation ask students for their reaction and comments. Discuss video and answer questions.

Definitions: Review definitions and incorporate into presentation.

Nursing Process: Focus on specifics of holistic assessment (Appendix 7–A) and intuitive thinking, nursing diagnoses (Exhibits 7–1 to 7–4), client outcomes, planning, implementation, and evaluation. Review Standards of Holistic Care (Appendix 1–A).

EXPERIENTIAL EXERCISES

(2 hours. Incorporation of sharing circles (see pp. 7 and 10) and experiential exercises is encouraged in class presentation. Refer to chapter section Specific Interventions for details.)

Holistic Assessment Tools: Have students compare current assessment tools from different clinical settings with the Holistic Assessment Tools (Appendixes 7–A and 7–B). Discuss the importance of a holistic assessment tool and how a holistic assessment tool can help in the identification of patient problems/needs more completely than a medical model systems assessment or head-to-toe assessment tool that may have a few psychosocial questions added.

Intuition: Explore intuition as an important aspect of a holistic assessment. Give examples from clinical practice. Invite students to share personal use of intuition or a felt sense that was noticed and led to insight or problem identification.

Nursing Process: Engage students in dynamics of the nursing process through case studies presentation using holistic assessment, intuitive thinking, nursing diagnoses, client outcomes, planning, implementation, and evaluation. Integrate nursing process discussion with the American Holistic Nurses' Association Standards of Holistic Nursing Practice (see Part II, standard XI).

ANNOTATED BIBLIOGRAPHY CARDS

Directions for Future Research: Have students choose one or more research questions as an area to explore for annotated bibliography cards. Encourage students to begin collecting articles that can support further investigation.

JOURNAL ENTRIES

Nurse Healer Reflections: Encourage students to use the chapter reflective questions as a guide to journal entries for exploring, understanding, and validating presence and healing.

ISIS

Nursing Research and Its Holistic Applications

CHAPTER OBJECTIVES

Refer to chapter for specific theory, clinical, and personal objectives. These will provide guidelines for the integration of objectives in class presentation, experiential sessions, and student homework assignments.

CHAPTER OVERVIEW

A significant body of research provides evidence of the enormous effects of consciousness on both health and illness. Investigators have shown that alternative therapies have the exciting potential to prevent illness and maintain high-level wellness. Such research has been instrumental in guiding the development of humanistic and holistic health care. The challenge for nursing is to apply these findings in nursing practice.

PROCESS EXERCISE #9

(15-minute opening experiential session using music and healing objects if desired)

Vision of Healing: Questioning the Rules of Science

Nurses have traditionally relied on accumulated practice experience as though it were synonymous with knowledge. Nothing is more effective in shaking this belief system loose than a confrontation with the fact that not everyone's experience leads to the same conclusion. It is when we explore new concepts and possibilities that we make breakthroughs into new clinical practice possibilities to improve the quality of care.

Begin with a guided relaxation exercise (5 minutes) and gradually fade in music of choice. Suggest to students that they can close their eyes or leave their eyes open. If eyes are open ask them to find a spot several feet in front of them to focus on. This allows for a greater ease in following the relaxation and imagery suggestions and reflective experience.

Using techniques for empowering relaxation and imagery scripts (see pp. 619–622), gently weave into a guided imagery exercise reflective questions such as these: How do I utilize research findings to guide my clinical practice? Do I have opportunities to try some of the current research findings? Do I have opportunities, but do not take advantage of them? Is there a research problem or interest area that I would like to explore? Add three to five more reflective questions about research. Bring closure to the imagery process.

With soft music still playing, invite students to record in a personal journal (3–5 minutes) any images, process questions and answers, or insight gained. Ask students to bring personal closure to this process. Gradually fade music out. Engage students in a gentle stretching exercise before the theory session begins.

KEY CONCEPTS: THEORY

(1-hour presentation)
OPTIONAL: GUEST SPEAKER(S) AND VIDEO(S)

Guest Speaker(s): Invite one or more nurses experienced in clinical research. Provide guest speaker(s) with the Instructor's Manual suggestion to become familiar with students' assignment before class.

Video(s): Show a video of a nurse researcher describing and demonstrating one or more aspects of clinical research (rent from media catalog or purchase for school video library). Following the video presentation ask students for their reaction and comments. Discuss video and answer questions.

Definitions: Review definitions and incorporate into presentation.

Wellness Model: Discuss how the framework of client/patient nursing research is shifting from an illness to a wellness model of health care.

Holistic Research Methods: Review the four categories and the six types of quantitative research. Discuss the purpose of quantitative research. Review the descriptive expressions of participants about the experience of health (Table 8–1).

Qualitative vs. Quantitative Research: Compare and contrast qualitative and quantitative methodologies (Table 8–2 and Table 8–3). Discuss how both methodologies are needed in holistic research.

Objectivity in Scientific Research: Discuss Heisenberg's Uncertainty Principle and its implications in holistic research. Discuss how certain phenomena related to holistic research may not be accessible to scientific investigation.

EXPERIENTIAL EXERCISES

(2 hours. Incorporation of sharing circles (see pp. 7 and 10) and experiential exercises is encouraged for class presentation.)

Holistic Measurement Tools: Review several research tools that measure a client's physical, mental, emotional, social, and spiritual dimensions.

The Placebo Response: Explore the placebo response. Discuss conditions and therapeutic procedures where the placebo response has been demonstrated. Cite clinical examples from your clinical practice or from the literature.

Evaluation of Alternative Therapies: Explore the types of research questions needed to evaluate alternative therapies, such as "What is the treatment of choice and under what circumstances should it be used?" Discuss the Office of Alternative Medicine (OAM) and review the current OAM-funded research studies.

Draft of a Research Proposal: Have students review the chapter section entitled Directions for Future Research as a guide for this exercise. Have students work in groups of 3–5 and draft a holistically oriented research design. Provide time for discussion and critiques of proposal drafts.

ANNOTATED BIBLIOGRAPHY CARDS

Directions for Future Research: Have students choose one or more research questions as an area to explore for annotated bibliography cards. Encourage students to begin collecting articles that can support further investigation.

JOURNAL ENTRIES

Nurse Healer Reflections: Encourage students to use chapter reflective questions as a guide to journal entries for exploring, understanding, and validating presence and healing.

UNIT III

MAXIMIZING HUMAN POTENTIAL

Chapter 9

Self-Assessments: Facilitating Healing in Self and Others

CHAPTER OBJECTIVES

Refer to chapter for specific theory, clinical, and personal objectives. These will provide guidelines for the integration of objectives in class presentation, experiential sessions, and student homework assignments.

CHAPTER OVERVIEW

Each of our human potentials affects our whole being. When one strives to develop all areas, a deeper sense of wholeness emerges, one's self-worth increases, and life goals are actualized. Being alive becomes more exciting, rewarding, and fulfilling. Even when frustrations arise, individuals who assess their human potentials can more easily recognize and make effective choices and decrease the barriers to maximizing human potentials.

PROCESS EXERCISE #9

(15-minute opening experiential session using music and healing objects if desired)

Vision of Healing: Actualization of Human Potentials

Our challenge in all aspects of our personal and professional lives is to strive to integrate all our human potentials. When we assess our human potentials and decide how we want our lives to be, we evoke meaning and purpose in life. If one area of our human potential is left undeveloped, life events do not seem to be as good as they could be.

Begin with a guided relaxation exercise (5 minutes) and gradually fade in music of choice. Suggest to students that they can close their eyes or leave their eyes open. If eyes are open ask them to find a spot several feet in front of them to focus on. This allows for a greater ease in following the relaxation and imagery suggestions and reflective experience.

Using techniques for empowering relaxation and imagery scripts (see pp. 619–622), gently weave into a guided imagery exercise reflective questions from each category of the human potential self-assessment. Imagine that you have a short period of time to share a healing moment and hurting moment with someone who loves you. Invite into your imagination a person who loves you unconditionally that is available to you to actively listen. How important is this to the healing process? What steps would you take to begin this process? Bring closure to the imagery process.

With soft music still playing, invite students to record in a personal journal (3–5 minutes) any images, process questions and answers, or insight gained. Ask students to bring personal closure to this process. Gradually fade music out. Engage students in a gentle stretching exercise before the theory session begins.

KEY CONCEPTS: THEORY

(1-hour presentation)

Definitions: Review definitions and incorporate into presentation.

Circle of Human Potential: Discuss the circle as an ancient symbol of wholeness and the constant interrelationship and interaction of all parts.

Development of Human Potentials: Develop the idea of body-mind-spirit as complex feedback loops that are in a constant state of change. Explore each dimension of human potential—physical, mental, emotions, relationships, choices, and spirit (Figure 9–1).

Description of Holistic Nursing and the Standards of Holistic Nursing Practice: Introduce the students to the American Holistic Nurses' Association (AHNA) description of Holistic Nursing and the AHNA Standards of Holistic Nursing Practice (Appendix 1–A). Focus on the importance of the Nurse-Focused Concepts and the Client/Patient-Focused Concepts.

EXPERIENTIAL EXERCISES

(2 hours. Incorporation of sharing circles (see pp. 7 and 10) and experiential exercises is encouraged for class presentation.)

Self-Assessments: Explore the importance of self-assessment as a means of developing health and clarity of purpose and meaning in life. Have students complete the self-assessments (Figures 9–2 to 9–7) and tabulate scores (Exhibit 9–1). Allow time for students to work in dyads and to share areas that are most challenging.

Affirmations: Guide students in an imagery exercise using several affirmations from each area of human potential (see boxes). Allow time for students to share experiences of affirming intentions and choices. Have students explore how affirmations can be of help in recognizing negative affirmations or changing a perception, attitude, belief, or value.

ANNOTATED BIBLIOGRAPHY CARDS

Directions for Future Research: Have students choose one or more research questions as an area to explore for annotated bibliography cards. Encourage students to begin collecting articles that can support further investigation.

JOURNAL ENTRIES

Nurse Healer Reflections: Encourage students to use chapter reflective questions as a guide to journal entries for exploring, understanding, and validating presence and healing.

Chapter 10

Cognitive Therapy

CHAPTER OBJECTIVES

Refer to chapter for specific theory, clinical, and personal objectives. These will assist with the integration of objectives in class presentation, experiential sessions, and guidelines for student homework assignments.

CHAPTER OVERVIEW

Thoughts can enter our consciousness uninvited and unplanned, but they wield a great influence over our bodymind. Both positive and negative thoughts and images can affect all body systems and physical and mental activity levels and expectations. Overcoming nonproductive lifelong behaviors can be challenging, but with careful choices of interventions and support from others, health-affirming change can take place.

PROCESS EXERCISE #10

(15-minute opening experiential session using music and healing objects if desired)

Vision of Healing: Changing Outcomes

Gently helping ourselves identify discrepancies between thoughts and reality allows us to bring the world into a clearer focus. By examining the silent dialogue that accompanies every interaction with the outer world, identifying false assumptions, distortions, and misinterpretations, we can choose to make healthy changes.

Begin with a guided relaxation exercise (5 minutes) and gradually fade in music of choice. Suggest to students that they can close their eyes or leave their eyes open. If eyes are open ask them to find a spot several feet in front of them to focus on. This allows for a greater ease in following the relaxation and imagery suggestions and reflective experience.

Using techniques for empowering relaxation and imagery scripts (pp. 619–622), gently weave into a guided imagery exercise reflective questions about cognitive distortion listed in the cognitive restructuring section. Following each distortion use the same distortion and create a cognitive restructuring. Engage students in feeling the internal experience within during the restructuring. Bring closure to the imagery process.

With soft music still playing, invite students to record in a personal journal (3–5 minutes) any images, process questions and answers, or insight gained. Ask students to bring personal closure to this process. Gradually fade music out. Engage students in a gentle stretching exercise before the theory session begins.

KEY CONCEPTS: THEORY

(1-hour presentation)
OPTIONAL: GUEST SPEAKERS(S) AND VIDEO(S)

Guest Speakers(s): Invite one or more nurses experienced in cognitive therapies. Provide guest speaker(s) with the Instructor's Manual suggestions to become familiar with students' assignment before class.

Video(s): Show a video of a practitioner who describes, demonstrates, and integrates one or more of the cognitive therapies (rent from local video store or media catalog or purchase for school video library). Following the video presentation ask students for their reaction and comments. Discuss video and answer questions.

Definitions: Review definitions and incorporate into presentation.

Cognitive Restructuring: Review the strategies and techniques and outcomes of cognitive restructuring. Focus on how these strategies and techniques help individuals reappraise and reassess their thinking and thinking errors and choose healthier alternatives. Describe seven cognitive errors, and give examples of each.

Goal Setting: Discuss goal setting. Determine the differences and similarities between client-generated and nurse-generated goals.

Contracting: Examine the components of a successful client–patient contract.

NURSING PROCESS

Focus on specifics of assessment, nursing diagnoses, client outcomes, planning, intervention, and evaluation (Table 10–1 and Exhibit 10–2). Instruct students in the importance of developing their style of preparation before, during, and at the end of the session.

EXPERIENTIAL EXERCISES

(2 hours. Incorporation of sharing circles (see pp. 7 and 10) and experiential exercises is encouraged in class presentation. Refer to chapter section Specific Interventions for details.)

Identification of Cognitive Distortions: Have students work in dyads and each identify a cognitive distortion. Next capture, replace, refute, or examine those distortions. Share these distortions and reflections.

Successful Goal Setting: Have students work in dyads and each identify a personal behavior that he or she wishes to change and write steps and goals to achieve the desired behavior. Have students contract with each other or choose another person that they respect to sign and date the contract.

Rewards for Achievements: Have students work in dyads and develop a list of meaningful rewards. Share the variety of rewards with each other.

Negotiation of Contracts: Before this class session, have each student enter into a contract about a desired health behavior change with another student or family member/significant other. After the end of a week review the contract and renegotiate the contract if necessary. Discuss the strengths and weaknesses of this contract and the contract process.

Case Study: Have students discuss case studies as well as incorporate a case study in group presentation. Encourage students to share other client/patient stories and to focus on the meaning of the stories, symptoms, illness, and use of specific symbols and metaphors.

49

ANNOTATED BIBLIOGRAPHY CARDS

Directions for Future Research: Have students choose one or more research questions as an area to explore for annotated bibliography cards. Encourage students to begin collecting articles that can support further investigation.

JOURNAL ENTRIES

Nurse Healer Reflections: Encourage students to use the chapter reflective questions as a guide to journal entries for exploring, understanding, and validating presence and healing.

Chapter 11

Nutrition, Exercise, and Movement

CHAPTER OBJECTIVES

Refer to chapter for specific theory, clinical, and personal objectives. These will assist with the integration of objectives in class presentation, experiential sessions, and student homework assignments.

CHAPTER OVERVIEW

Joy and vitality can come from eating well, exercising regularly, and moving creatively to the rhythm of life. The lack of these health habits contribute to major risk factors for disease. As nurses better understand the challenges and dynamics of nutrition, exercise, and movement, they can more effectively assess clients, assist them with lifestyle changes, and provide them with guidelines to sustain healthier lifestyle habits.

PROCESS EXERCISE #11

(15-minute opening experiential session using music and healing objects if desired)

Vision of Healing: Nourishing the Bodymind

Nutrition and exercise work synergistically to promote high-level wellness. Food consumption and physical activity have a direct effect on the body, mind, and spirit. In general, the feeling of well-being that comes from physical health permeates all of our activities, enables quicker mental thought processes, allows for more restful sleep, and facilitates relaxation that leads to a deeper spiritual understanding.

Begin with a guided relaxation exercise (5 minutes) and gradually fade in music of choice. Suggest to students that they can close their eyes or leave them open. If eyes are left open ask them to find a spot several feet in front of them to focus on. This allows for a greater ease in following the suggestions and reflective experience.

Using techniques for empowering relaxation and imagery scripts (pp. 619–622), gently weave into a guided imagery exercise reflective questions about images of an ideal body that is personally right for the individual. Invite students to imagine standing in front of a mirror and seeing and thinking how they might appear if they were eating and moving at optimum levels. Direct them to consider their body dimensions, posture, flexibility, strength potential, skin and hair texture, and other aspects that directly relate to nutrition and exercise. Bring closure to the imagery process.

With soft music still playing, invite students to record in a personal journal (3–5 minutes) any images, process questions and answers, or insight gained. Ask students to bring personal closure to this process. Gradually fade music out. Engage students in a gentle stretching exercise before the theory session begins.

KEY CONCEPTS: THEORY

(1-hour presentation)
OPTIONAL: GUEST SPEAKERS(S) AND VIDEO(S)

Guest Speaker(s): Invite one or more nurses experienced in nutrition, exercise, and movement counseling. Provide the guest speaker(s) with Instructor's Manual suggestions to become familiar with students' assignment before class.

Video(s): Show a video of a practitioner who describes, demonstrates, and integrates nutrition, exercise, and movement (rent from media catalog or purchase for school video library). Following the video presentation ask students for their reaction and comments. Discuss video and answer questions.

Definitions: Review definitions and incorporate into presentation.

Theory and Research about Nutrition: Review current concepts and research findings in the areas of general nutrition, chronic disease and food, cancer, osteoporosis, populations with special needs, older adults, and athletes.

Current Nutrition Recommendations: Discuss the Food Guide Pyramid (Figure 11–1) and Mediterranean Diet Pyramid (Figure 11–2). Compare and contrast these two food guides. Discuss the dietary goals and recommendations (Table 11–1).

Alternative and Supplementary Food Sources: Discuss alternative and nontraditional foods. Review fat and water soluble vitamins (Table 11–1) and macrominerals and trace elements (Table 11–3).

Exercise: Discuss traditional exercise programs and exercise needs in special situations and with certain health conditions.

Movement: Review movement therapies and how they broaden the scope and choices of available exercise programs.

NURSING PROCESS

Focus on specifics of assessment, nursing diagnoses, client outcomes, planning, intervention, and evaluation (Table 11–4 and Exhibit 11–1). Instruct students in importance of developing their style of preparation before, during, and at the end of the session.

EXPERIENTIAL EXERCISES

(2 hours. Incorporation of sharing circles (see pp. 7 and 10) and experiential exercises is encouraged for class presentation. Refer to chapter section entitled Specific Interventions for details.)

Assessing Where I Am Now: Often we cannot remember what we ate or how much movement we incorporated into our life even as recently as yesterday. Before we can adequately assess how well we are addressing nutrition and exercise needs, we need to examine our past behaviors. Ask students to refer to homework assignments on Self-Assessments and the Circle of Human Potential (Chapter 9).

Cholesterol-Lowering Diet: Ask students to review the cholesterol-lowering diet. Discuss how the cholesterol-lowering diet can be incorporated into a personal dietary plan. Explore different teaching strategies for decreased fat intake.

Exercise: Review the three key points of an exercise program. Ask students to self-design a program that will work for them. Consider how and in what settings this information is introduced to clients.

Movement: Review the four components of creative movement: centering, warm-up, exploration of surrounding space, and stretching. Incorporate stretching and movement exercises in class.

Case Study: Have students discuss case studies as well as incorporate a case study in group presentation. Encourage students to share other client/patient stories and to focus on the meaning of the symptoms, disease, illness, and use of specific symbols and metaphors.

ANNOTATED BIBLIOGRAPHY CARDS

Directions for Future Research: Have students choose one or more research questions as an area to explore for annotated bibliography cards. Encourage students to begin collecting articles that can support further investigation.

JOURNAL ENTRIES

Nurse Healer Reflections: Encourage students to use the chapter reflective questions as a guide to journal entries for exploring, understanding, and validating presence and healing.

Chapter 12

Environment: Protecting Our Personal and Planetary Home

CHAPTER OBJECTIVES

Refer to chapter for specific theory, clinical, and personal objectives. These will assist with the integration of objectives in class presentation, experiential sessions, and student homework assignments.

CHAPTER OVERVIEW

Environment and its many uses are among the foremost issues of the 1990s. Nurses are emerging as leaders in the education of others about the benefit of working together to protect and enhance personal and community environmental spaces. The air we breathe, the sounds we hear, and the space we see all affect how we feel, think, and function.

PROCESS EXERCISE #12

(15-minute opening experiential session using music and healing objects if desired)

Vision of Healing: Building a Healthy Environment

As we explore our personal environments we become increasingly aware of the effects of our actions and behaviors upon the whole planet. On an individual level, the way in which people use their personal space affects not only the way they feel, but also, in today's shrinking world, the space around others.

Begin with a guided relaxation exercise (5 minutes) and gradually fade in music of choice. Suggest to students that they can close their eyes or leave their eyes open. If eyes are left open ask them to find a spot several feet in front of them to focus on. This allows for a greater ease in following the suggestions and reflective experience.

Using techniques for empowering relaxation and imagery scripts (see pp. 619–622), gently weave into a guided imagery exercise reflective questions about the space in which they currently live and work. Have the students reflect on the esthetics, the aromas, the sound, and the sight of their environment. Ask them to consider what a healing environment would be like. Bring closure to the imagery process.

With soft music still playing, invite students to record in a personal journal (3–5 minutes) any images, process questions and answers, or insight gained. Ask students to bring personal closure to this process. Gradually fade music out. Engage students in a gentle stretching exercise before the theory session begins.

KEY CONCEPTS: THEORY

(1-hour presentation)
OPTIONAL: GUEST SPEAKER(S) AND VIDEO(S)

Guest Speaker(s): Invite one or more nurses experienced in environmental issues. Provide guest speaker(s) with Instructor's Manual suggestions to become familiar with student's assignment before class.

Video(s): Show a video about environmental issues (rent from local video store or media catalog or purchase for school video library). Following the video presentation ask students for their reaction and comments. Discuss video and answer questions.

Definitions: Review definitions and incorporate into presentation.

The Modern Dilemma: Review current environmental concerns (Figure 12–1). Discuss how this model affects everyone. Ask for suggestions of how each individual's personal change can make a difference.

Noise: Explore how noise may be one of the most common environmental health hazards. Discuss the physiological and psychological effects of noise pollution and steps to help correct noise pollution.

Food Irradiation: Discuss both positive and negative effects of the controversial food irradiation treatment program.

Meat and Poultry Supplementation: Have an open discussion on the pros and cons of this program. Include the most recent new information to augment discussion.

Passive Smoking: Engage students in discussion of situations where the documented environmental passive smoking hazard affects them on a daily basis. Ask students to consider strategies to decrease this health hazard in their personal and work environments.

Violence, Dehumanization, and the Technologic Age: Contrast urban, suburban, and rural environmental safety facts in your area. Discuss the potential hazards of technology and how to reduce them.

Nurses' Work Environment: Discuss a variety of health care delivery environments such as acute care, long-term care, and home health care. Encourage the students to identify potential environmental hazards and possible ways to correct or avoid them.

NURSING PROCESS

Focus on specifics of assessment, nursing diagnoses, client outcomes, planning, intervention, and evaluation (Table 12–2 and Exhibit 12–1). Instruct students in the importance of developing their style of preparation before, during, and at the end of the session.

EXPERIENTIAL EXERCISES

(2 hours. Incorporation of sharing circles (see pp. 7 and 10) and experiential exercises is encouraged for class presentation. Refer to chapter section entitled Specific Interventions for details.)

Personal Environment: Engage students in a reflective experience of bringing to their mind their personal living space and the healing aspects as well as those aspects that are not healing. Have students briefly share their experience and also share what was learned from sharing with others. In another guided imagery exercise, ask students to listen carefully to all the sounds in their current environment, then open eyes. Follow the suggested steps for recording and analyzing what was heard.

Workplace Hazards: Discuss workplace hazards. Follow the suggested steps (Table 12–3) to identify possible problems and solutions.

Planetary Consciousness: Develop a guided imagery and music exercise with a central focus/theme of interconnectedness of working together to enhance our planetary home. This allows students to deepen their experience of creating their own special place in the universe and how each person's individual actions work together to create the whole.

Case Study: Have students discuss case studies as well as incorporate a case study in group presentation. Encourage students to share other client/patient stories and to focus on the meaning of the symptoms, disease, illness, and use of specific symbols and metaphors.

ANNOTATED BIBLIOGRAPHY CARDS

Directions for Future Research: Have students choose one or more research questions as an area to explore for annotated bibliography cards. Encourage students to begin collecting articles that can support further investigation.

JOURNAL ENTRIES

Nurse Healer Reflections: Encourage students to use the chapter reflective questions as a guide to journal entries for exploring, understanding, and validating presence and healing.

Chapter 13

Play and Laughter: Moving Toward Harmony

CHAPTER OBJECTIVES

Refer to chapter for specific theory, clinical, and personal objectives. These will assist with the integration of objectives in class presentation, experiential sessions, and student homework assignments.

CHAPTER OVERVIEW

Whether helping ourselves or clients through difficult procedures or strengthening our ability to move smoothly through a shift assignment, humor and playfulness help keep us centered and whole. Humor can help us tap into the spiritual and evolutionary possibilities inherent in all events.

PROCESS EXERCISE #13

(15-minute opening experiential session using music and healing objects if desired)

Vision of Healing: Releasing the Energy of the Playful Child

Play is part of the richness of life; it enables us to live and grow. As infants and children, we play to learn. As adults, we play to relax, to enjoy interaction with others, to grow, and to gain a different perspective on our lives. Our play can be a variety of activities, from the simple experience of skipping or dancing for the joy of movement to the excitement of "playing to win" in a tournament or game.

Begin with a guided relaxation exercise (5 minutes) and gradually fade in music of choice. Suggest to students that they can close their eyes or leave their eyes open. If eyes are open ask them to find a spot several feet in front of them to focus on. This allows for a greater ease in following the relaxation and imagery suggestions and reflective experience.

Using techniques for empowering relaxation and imagery scripts (pp. 619–622), gently weave into a guided imagery exercise reflective questions and ask students to remember an event or time where spontaneous hilarity was present. Encourage them to engage in the moment remembering as many details as possible using all of their senses. Invite them to laugh out loud as they evoke this special memory. Bring closure to the imagery process.

With soft music still playing, invite students to record in a personal journal (3–5 minutes) any images, process questions and answers, or insight gained. Ask students to bring personal closure to this process. Gradually fade music out. Engage students in a gentle stretching exercise before the theory session begins.

KEY CONCEPTS: THEORY

(1-hour presentation)
OPTIONAL: GUEST SPEAKERS(S) AND VIDEO(S)

Guest Speakers(s): Invite a nurse or clown experienced in play and laughter therapies. Provide guest speaker with the Instructor's Manual suggestions to become familiar with students' assignment before class.

Video(s): Show a video that evokes play and laughter (rent from local video store or media catalog or purchase for school video library). Following the video presentation ask students for their reaction and comments. Discuss video and answer questions.

Definitions: Review definitions and incorporate into presentation.

Play in Ancient Cultures: Discuss play from a historical perspective.

Play in Today's Society: Examine the difference between "pure play" and "winning."

Bodymind Connections and Play and Laughter: Review the research on play and laughter and the relationships between health and healing.

Laughter and Humor as Coping Responses: Examine how play and laughter allow individuals to forgive themselves for imperfections, mistakes, and failures.

Play and the Adult: Discuss how adults often become constrained and reserved both literally and figuratively. Explore how play and laughter often require development as individuals mature.

Playfulness in the Work Environment: Explore how a shift in attitude at work can allow an individual to feel freedom and to "recharge the battery."

NURSING PROCESS

Focus on specifics of assessment, nursing diagnoses, client outcomes, planning, intervention, and evaluation (Table 13–1 and Exhibit 13–1). Instruct students in the importance of developing their style of preparation before, during, and at the end of the session.

EXPERIENTIAL EXERCISES

(2 hours. Incorporation of sharing circles (see pp. 7 and 10) and experiential exercises is encouraged in class presentation. Refer to chapter section Specific Interventions for details.)

Cultivating Spontaneous Silliness: Have students work in dyads and identify times during the day when they play with a sense of freedom and without guilt, rather than competing.

Playing Games: Have students work in groups of 3–5 and spontaneously come up with a game in a few minutes. For example, practice laughing out loud until a deep clear "belly laugh" is heard from everyone. Then engage the rest of the class in the playfulness of the game. Share in a group the play strategies used in a day to decrease the stress of responsibility and work.

Collecting Cartoons: Prior to this class, ask students to collect a few cartoons that are humorous. Spend time in class sharing cartoons and assess the variety of humor and satire.

Using Humorous Books, Audiotapes, and Videotapes: Prior to this class review at least one humorous book, audiotape, or video. Bring a reference to class and explore how easy it is for a group to create a humor library. Discuss the articles included and determine what categories they can be placed in and if they might be more effective for certain groups of clients or patients.

Case Study: Have students discuss case studies as well as incorporate a case study in group presentation. Encourage students to share other client/patient stories and to focus on meaning of the stories, symptoms, illness, and use of specific symbols and metaphors.

ANNOTATED BIBLIOGRAPHY CARDS

Directions for Future Research: Have students choose one or more research questions as an area to explore for annotated bibliography cards. Encourage students to begin collecting articles that can support further investigation.

JOURNAL ENTRIES

Nurse Healer Reflections: Encourage students to use the chapter reflective questions as a guide to journal entries for exploring, understanding, and validating presence and healing.

Chapter 14

Self-Reflection: Consulting the Truth Within

CHAPTER OBJECTIVES

Refer to chapter for specific theory, clinical, and personal objectives. These will assist with the integration of objectives in class presentation, experiential sessions, and student homework assignments.

CHAPTER OVERVIEW

Self-reflection interventions are strategies for discovering one's inner wisdom that is often buried during daily routines. These interventions differ from most client education modules in that the learning comes from inner knowledge and is primarily client-generated. These strategies assist all individuals to reach for higher levels of wellness and understanding of the life process. Self-reflection can be successfully woven into the fabric of both professional and personal life.

PROCESS EXERCISE #14

(15-minute opening experiential session using music and healing objects if desired)

Vision of Healing: Healthy Disclosure

As nurses, we can refresh our own self-reflection techniques and perfect new ones to help us record and grow from our experiences, intuitions, and connections. Self-reflection helps us to evoke more trust and truth in daily life.

Begin with a guided relaxation exercise (5 minutes) and gradually fade in music of choice. Suggest to students that they can close their eyes or leave their eyes open. If eyes are open ask them to find a spot several feet in front of them to focus on. This allows for a greater ease in following the relaxation and imagery suggestions and reflective experience.

Using techniques for empowering relaxation and imagery scripts (pp. 619–622), gently weave into a guided imagery exercise the parable in the Vision of Healing. Using the metaphors from the parable create several reflective questions about truth and invite students to access and explore a deep truth that is important in their life. Bring closure to the imagery process.

With soft music still playing, invite students to record in a personal journal (3–5 minutes) any images, process questions and answers, or insight gained. Ask students to bring personal closure to this process. Gradually fade music out. Engage students in an easy stretching exercise before the theory session is begun.

KEY CONCEPTS: THEORY

(1-hour presentation)
OPTIONAL: GUEST SPEAKERS(S) AND VIDEO(S)

Guest Speakers(s): Invite one or more nurses experienced in self-reflection interventions. Provide guest speaker(s) with Instructor's Manual suggestions to become familiar with students' assignment before class.

Video(s): Show a video of a practitioner who describes, demonstrates, and integrates one or more of the self-reflection therapies (rent from a media catalog or purchase for school video library). Following the video presentation ask students for their reaction and comments. Discuss video and answer questions.

Definitions: Review definitions and incorporate into presentation.

Self-Reflection: Provide a broad overview of self-reflection. Review the four ways in which adults learn and how the adult learning process differs from how children learn. Incorporate within the discussion self-concept, experience, problem solving, and applicability of knowledge.

Connections: Review how self-reflection acts as an intermediary between the various aspects and expressions of the bodymind. Discuss specific hemispheric function and the importance of both logic and nonlogical ways of knowing.

Reconnecting with Life Events: Discuss how self-reflection interventions help an individual reconnect with events, reinterpret the actions and emotions connected with those events, and reframe their physiologic and emotional experiences. Introduce self-reflection interventions of diaries, journals, and letters.

Drawing on Intuition: Discuss the Latin origin of the word *intuition*. Incorporate discussion of intuition with the hemispheric function of logic and nonlogical ways of knowing.

Understanding Dreams: Explore dreams as a self-reflection tool.

Telling Stories: Discuss the different types of stories such as fairy tales, myths, mystery novels, movies, family anecdotes, remembrances. Explore the profound events that can occur when two or more individuals tell and share special healing moments and stories.

Reminiscing and Embarking on a Life Review: Develop the three components of reminiscing—memory, experience, and social interaction.

NURSING PROCESS

Focus on specifics of assessment, nursing diagnoses, client outcomes, planning, intervention, and evaluation (Table 14–1 and Exhibit 14–3). Instruct students in the importance of developing their style of preparation before, during, and at the end of the session.

EXPERIENTIAL EXERCISES

(2 hours. Incorporation of sharing circles (see pp. 7 and 10) and experiential exercises is encouraged in class presentation. Refer to chapter section Specific Interventions for details.)

Keeping Diaries and Journals: Prior to this class have students select a special writing pen, paper, or notebook that will be brought to and used in each class session as well as used for the journaling assignment (5 minutes each day) out of class. Encourage students to explore Progoff's categories and divisions for keeping a journal. Explore the usefulness of a structured client diary (Exhibit 14–1 and 14–2) and how individuals can gain insight about symptom pattern awareness, healing (negative) thoughts and images, the impact of interventions used, and the amount of pain medications taken in relationship to daily events.

Writing Letters: Have students write a letter to another person that expresses some deep emotions that may have been kept inside (e.g., unconditional love, forgiveness, remembrances, anger, disappointment, etc.).

Beginning an Intuition Log: Encourage students to carry a small notebook in their pocket and to record each time they have a hunch or flash of insight, hear a quiet, inner voice, or sense a vague impression or feeling. Have students share some insights in the next class session.

Learning from Dreams: Review the reflective questions about dream content for interpretation and clarification. Invite students to practice the lucid dreaming guidelines during the semester. Encourage students to keep a portion of a personal journal for dreams.

Building Mind Maps and Clusters: Review the process of clustering (Figure 14–1). Have students work in small groups. In the center of a piece of paper write the words "healing environment." Next have students create a mind map and clusters for a healing environment on another piece of paper. Ask the students to identify an area of their life, a project, or a relationship where they feel stuck. Ask them to create a cluster of ways to increase creativity and problem solving (e.g., people, ideas, solutions, etc.).

Sharing Stories: Have students work in triads and, beginning with "Once upon a time," tell a story about an actual event or one created in the moment. Provide time for sharing stories.

Using Reminiscence and Life Review: Explore the life review process. Prior to this class, ask students to do a life review with a child and with a senior citizen. Search for similarities and differences between children and older adults.

Case Study: Have students discuss case studies as well as incorporate a case study in group presentation. Encourage students to share other client/patient stories and to focus on the meaning of symptoms, disease, illness, and the use of specific symbols and metaphors.

ANNOTATED BIBLIOGRAPHY CARDS

Directions for Future Research: Have students choose one or more research questions as an area to explore for annotated bibliography cards. Encourage students to begin collecting articles that can support further investigation.

JOURNAL ENTRIES

Nurse Healer Reflections: Encourage students to use the chapter reflective questions as a guide to journal entries for exploring, understanding, and validating presence and healing.

Chapter 15

Relationships: Learning the Patterns and Processes

CHAPTER OBJECTIVES

Refer to chapter for specific theory, clinical, and personal objectives. These will provide guidelines for the integration of objectives in class presentation, experiential sessions, and student homework assignments.

CHAPTER OVERVIEW

Healthy relationships increase health and wholeness. Healthy relationships help us to understand at a deep level our interconnectedness with people, nature, and the universe. When we are in healthy relationships, we exhibit mutual love, sharing, and the ability to forgive ourselves and others. As nurses focus on family systems theory and relationship patterns, they can counsel and empower individuals more effectively in leaning healing strategies within the context of relationships.

PROCESS EXERCISE #15

(15-minute opening experiential session using music and healing objects if desired)

Vision of Healing: Accepting Ourselves and Others

Wholeness and healing can exist only when we have meaningful relationships. The extent to which we are willing to accept ourselves determines the quality of relationships. A relationship is healing if it nurtures expression of feelings, needs, and desires and if it helps remove barriers to love.

Begin with a guided relaxation exercise (5 minutes) and gradually fade in music of choice. Suggest to students that they can close their eyes or leave their eyes open. If eyes are open ask them to find a spot several feet in front of them to focus on. This allows for a greater ease in following the relaxation and imagery suggestions and reflective experience.

Using techniques for empowering relaxation and imagery scripts (pp. 619–622), gently weave into a guided imagery exercise the reflective questions from the Vision of Healing to increase awareness of current patterns in their relationships and to identify the relationships that are in need of healing. Pace these questions to allow time for images, emotions, and other responses. Bring closure to the imagery process.

With soft music still playing, invite students to record in a personal journal (3–5 minutes) any images, process questions and answers, or insight gained. Ask students to bring personal closure to this process. Gradually fade music out. Engage students in a gentle stretching exercise before the theory session begins.

KEY CONCEPTS: THEORY

(1-hour presentation)
OPTIONAL: GUEST SPEAKER(S) AND VIDEO(S)

Guest Speaker(s): Invite one or more nurses who have a family counseling practice to discuss the dynamics of family counseling. Provide guest speaker(s) with the Instructor's Manual suggestion to become familiar with students' assignment before class.

Video(s): Show a video of a practitioner describing and demonstrating one or more holistic modalities in family counseling (rent from media catalog or purchase for school video library). Following the video presentation ask students for their reaction and comments. Discuss video and answer questions.

Definitions: Review definitions and incorporate into presentation.

Patterns in Family Systems and Relationships: Discuss how the sequences, patterns, simultaneous events, and circular reactions that occur within a family create the dynamics for a healthy or unhealthy family system. Review the example given within a family of four and the multiple relationships and the complex reverberating feedback loop that can occur.

Characteristics of Systems: Explore family systems characteristics and the difference in an open family/relationship system and a closed family/relationship system.

Defenses in Relationships: Review denial, projection, rationalization, reaction formation, repression, and regression. Give examples of each.

The Ultradian Family: Review the basic rest–activity cycle of ultradian rhythms. Summarize the major links of ultradian rhythms to family health, harmony, and healing in relationships.

NURSING PROCESS

Focus on specifics of assessment, nursing diagnoses, client outcomes, planning, intervention, and evaluation (Table 15–1 and Exhibit 15–2). Instruct students in importance of developing their style of preparation before, during, and at the end of the session.

EXPERIENTIAL EXERCISES

(2 hours. Incorporation of sharing circles (see pp. 7 and 10) and experiential exercises is encouraged for presentation. Refer to chapter section entitled Specific Interventions for details.)

Counseling and Psychotherapy: Review the common counseling strategies (Table 15–2). Have students work in dyads. Discuss different clinical situations where they have used several of the strategies listed. Share specific situations where psychotherapy was indicated and the client was referred to a counselor, psychotherapist, etc.

Storytelling: Review the guidelines that enhance the use of stories as therapy. Have students work in dyads. The first student will tell a personal story and connect one story to the next. The student that has been listening will share the story themes that bridged from one story to the next. The listener will reflect on what part of the story was not being told with as much depth as other parts. Have students switch roles of sharing and listening.

Intimacy Awareness, "I" Statements, and Stem Phrase Completion: Review Case Study No. 1, which integrates these exercises. Follow guidelines and questions for each of these exercises. Have students work in dyads. Have one student begin the first exercise while the other student listens. Switch roles after each exercise. Encourage students to answer quickly with each response and not to analyze answers (Exhibit 15–1).

Development of Spiritual Understanding: Encourage students to review the developmental process guidelines for gaining spiritual understanding. Next have students assess what strategies they currently use each day and what additional strategies would be helpful in deepening their spiritual understanding.

Ways to Work through Fear: Review the three levels of fear. Have students work in dyads and share a fear with each other. Ask students to identify the fear level that has been shared. After each student has shared a fear, the student that has been listening can read the five truths to help the student deal with the fear.

Improved Communication: Have students work in dyads. The first student will access a stressful event in his or her life and will also access emotions of the event within the body (physiologic responses of heart beat, shallow breathing, cold hands, body tension, etc.) as the story is told. The student that is listening is to observe any body language that reflects emotions. Discuss after each student tells a stressful event. Blood pressure cuffs, hand thermometers, or biofeedback equipment can be used before, during, and after the communication to demonstrate the dramatic and frequent changes in dialogue.

Focusing: Review the five focusing skills and five focusing steps (Figure 15–1). Have students work in dyads. This exercises helps individuals become more aware of the bodymind wisdom, the felt sense, and increase skills of intuition. The student that serves as the guide will not know the experience of the student going through the focusing steps until the end of the five steps or several rounds of the focusing exercise. Have students share the experience. Have students switch roles. Each student may require several rounds of focusing before recognizing the inner sensations.

Empty Chair: Demonstrate this exercise to the group at large. Ask for student volunteers that want to experience the exercise. Refer to Case Study No. 2.

Case Study: Have students discuss case studies (see Figure 15–2 to 15–4) as well as incorporate a case study in group presentation. Encourage sharing of other client/patient stories focusing on the meaning of the stories, symptoms, illness, and use of specific symbols and metaphors.

ANNOTATED BIBLIOGRAPHY CARDS

Directions for Future Research: Have students choose one or more research questions as an area to explore for annotated bibliography cards. Encourage students to begin collecting articles that can support further investigation.

JOURNAL ENTRIES

Nurse Healer Reflections: Encourage students to use the chapter reflective questions as a guide to journal entries for exploring, understanding, and validating presence and healing.

Chapter 16

Sexual Abuse: Healing the Wounds

CHAPTER OBJECTIVES

Refer to chapter for specific theory, clinical, and personal objectives. These will assist with the integration of objectives in class presentation, experiential sessions, and student homework assignments.

CHAPTER OVERVIEW

Working with survivors of abuse of violence is one of the most difficult experiences, but it is also one of the most rewarding. Because of a reluctance to inquire, it is possible to work with a client over a long period of time without knowing that he or she has been or may even still be involved in a violent situation.

PROCESS EXERCISE #16

(15-minute opening experiential session using music and healing objects if desired)

Vision of Healing: Recovering the Self and Maintaining the Self

The recovery of the self moves in cycles and layers. Both client and nurse must be prepared for this circuitous journey to wholeness, taking each new stage as reassurance of progress.

Begin with a guided relaxation exercise (5 minutes) and gradually fade in music of choice. Suggest to students that they can close their eyes or leave their eyes open. If eyes are open ask them to find a spot several feet in front of them to focus on. This allows for a greater ease in following the relaxation and imagery suggestions and reflective experience.

Using techniques for empowering relaxation and imagery scripts (pp. 619–622), gently weave into a guided imagery exercise reflective questions using an artichoke as a metaphor of the self. To get to the heart of the artichoke, we must peel away layer after layer. To get to our own heart, we must go below the outer surface to discover our essential core of healing.

Invite students to begin to peel away the outer layer of burdens, problems, and begin to go below the surface, deep into the self, to find the inner healing resources that are present within the moment to bring about healing. In the imagination have students complete these sentences: "The part of me that is most in need of healing in this moment is.... The thing that I can do in this moment to bring about the healing is...." Bring closure to the imagery process.

With soft music still playing, invite students to record in a personal journal (3–5 minutes) any images, process questions and answers, or insight gained. Ask students to bring personal closure to this process. Gradually fade music out. Engage students in a gentle stretching exercise before the theory session begins.

KEY CONCEPTS: THEORY

(1-hour presentation)
OPTIONAL: GUEST SPEAKER(S) AND VIDEO(S)

Guest Speaker(s): Ask one or more sexual abuse counselors to address precautions when working with survivors, bodymind responses, the TRIADs Assessment Tool, and moving through memories. Provide guest speaker(s) with the Instructor's Manual suggestions to become familiar with students' assignment before class.

Video(s): Review a video that explores the dynamics of using holistic modalities in sexual abuse counseling.

Definitions: Review definitions and incorporate into presentation.

Precautions When Working with Survivors: Discuss the phenomenon of repressed memories and ways to avoid imposing one's suspicions of abuse on a client's memory gaps. Provide students with counselors, support groups, and referral sources for survivors and perpetrators of abuse in your community.

Bodymind Responses: Discuss the post-traumatic stress disorder as a model for the symptoms of sexual abuse and approaches to treatment. Explore the possible physical, emotional, and behavioral consequences of child as well as adult abuse.

The TRIADs Assessment Tool: Discuss the TRIADs Assessment Tool and its application to different types of abuse such as sexual abuse, domestic violence, ethnic/gay/hate assaults, child abuse, and cult torture. Discuss different ways to incorporate questions concerning abuse into the client interview format.

Moving through Memories: Discuss the tradition therapeutic interventions, including individual and support groups, as well as the emerging adjunctive interventions that incorporate expressive arts such as drawing, psychodrama, movement, journaling, and anger expression workout.

NURSING PROCESS

Focus on specifics of assessment, nursing diagnoses, client outcomes, planning, intervention, and evaluation (Table 16–1 and Exhibit 16–1). Instruct students in the importance of developing their style of preparation before, during, and at the end of the session.

EXPERIENTIAL EXERCISES

(2 hours. Incorporation of sharing circles (see pp. 7 and 10) and experiential exercises is encouraged in class presentation. Refer to chapter section Specific Interventions for details.)

Grounding Skills: Explore dissociation that may happen with painful memories and how dissociation may prevent survivors from recognizing dangerous situations, making them more vulnerable to further victimization. Have students share different grounding strategies to use for self or others to stay present rather than to become overwhelmed by a memory.

Relaxation: Examine how disturbing flashbacks and body memories may surface when the physical armor of tension is quieted. Explore how individuals may equate relaxation with vulnerability that conflicts with their hyperviligence. Discuss the best relaxation strategies for abuse survivors.

Imagery: Explore how imagery can be used as a healing modality to assist the abuse survivor to connect with the suppressed emotions surrounding the abuse experience as well as to be face to face with the perpetrator in the imagination. Review the imagery process steps discussed in the text of acting "as if," that is, having the client get in touch with the somatic response, and be face to face with the perpetrator. As the client rehearses this event in a safe, structured environment, a situation is created for the person to move beyond the pain, anger, and sadness of the situation.

Biofeedback: Examine biofeedback as a strategy for helping abuse survivors connect with body sensations and gain control over uncomfortable physiologic responses. Discuss the precautions when working with different types of abuse survivors.

Hypnosis and Self-Hypnosis: Explore how hypnosis and self-hypnosis is a structured process of relaxation designed to produce a state of dissociation that facilitates an individual's ability to get in touch with unconscious parts of the self, such as feeling, memories, or awareness.

Bodywork: Explore how bodywork is a means for abuse survivors to learn to reconnect to their body responses, to provide a path to the retrieval of memories, and to speed the retrieval of memories and the recovery of body sensations.

Writing: Encourage students to prepare a family record and note the presence of any perpetrators or victims of violence or members with substance abuse or eating disorders. If painful memories or associations occur with any of the students, encourage them to learn healing strategies and to seek out assistance and resolution of painful memories with a nurse therapist or join a support group that is under the guidance of a trained counselor.

Art Therapy: Review the work of art therapists or sexual abuse counselors who have used art, collages, photography, clay, masks, etc., to tap into deep feelings and understanding that are inaccessible to the verbal realm alone. Discuss recurring themes, symbols, colors, or objects that give personal clues to memory fragments or thoughts that are not yet safe to put into words.

Video Therapy: Review or develop policies and procedures for dealing with the emotional and physical needs of victims of abuse in emergency situations or other clinical situations. Discuss the five-stage process of video disclosure.

Anger Expression and Management: Have students work in groups of 3–5 and share their personal style of anger management that allows expression of anger without injury to self or others.

Case Study: Have students discuss case studies as well as incorporate a case study in group presentation. Encourage students to share other client/patient stories and to focus on the meaning of symptoms, disease, illness, and use of specific symbols and metaphors.

ANNOTATED BIBLIOGRAPHY CARDS

Directions for Future Research: Have students choose one or more research questions as an area to explore for annotated bibliography cards. Encourage students to begin collecting articles that can support further investigation.

JOURNAL ENTRIES

Nurse Healer Reflections: Encourage students to use the chapter reflective questions as a guide to journal entries for exploring, understanding, and validating presence and healing.

Chapter 17

Peaceful Deathing and Death

CHAPTER OBJECTIVES

Refer to chapter for specific theory, clinical, and personal objectives. These will provide guidelines for the integration of objectives in class presentation, experiential sessions, and student homework assignments.

CHAPTER OVERVIEW

Caring for and counseling a dying person and the family/significant others is an art, and the art of peaceful living and peaceful deathing and dying is the same. When preparation is made (e.g., relaxation, imagery, co-meditation, etc., are learned), deathing can be a series of conscious, spirit-filled, light-filled moments that lead to the ultimate peaceful moment of death. The more we integrate solitude, inward-focused practice, and conscious awareness into daily life, the more peaceful is the deathing process and the moment of death.

PROCESS EXERCISE #17

(15-minute opening experiential session using music and other healing objects if desired)

Vision of Healing: Releasing Attachment

Nothing in life prepares us for our own death and the death of loved ones. True healing and deathing in peace come from integrating the creative process and art of healing into our daily lives.

Begin with a guided relaxation exercise (5 minutes) and gradually fade in music of choice. Suggest to students that they can close their eyes or leave their eyes open. If eyes are open ask them to find a spot several feet in front of them to focus on. This allows for a greater ease in following the relaxation and imagery suggestions and reflective experience.

Using techniques for empowering relaxation and imagery scripts (pp. 619–622), gently weave into a guided relaxation and imagery exercise reflective scripts for deathing in peace—*Letting Go, Opening the Heart, and Forgiving Self and Others.* Bring closure to the imagery process.

With soft music still playing, invite students to record in a personal journal (3–5 minutes) any images, process questions and answers, or insight gained. Ask students to bring personal closure to this process. Gradually fade music out. Engage students in a gentle stretching exercise before the theory session begins.

KEY CONCEPTS: THEORY

(1-hour presentation)
OPTIONAL: GUEST SPEAKER(S) AND VIDEO(S)

Guest Speaker(s): Invite one or more hospice nurses to discuss holistic modalities that are used with individuals in various stages of deathing and grieving. Provide guest speaker(s) with the Instructor's Manual suggestions to become familiar with students' assignment before class.

Video(s): Show a video about the deathing or grieving process (rent from media catalog or purchase for school video library). Following the video presentation ask students for their reaction and comments. Discuss video and answer questions.

Definitions: Review definitions and incorporate into presentation.

Myths and Beliefs: Explore how myths are our storylines, beliefs, and images. Discuss the five-stage program on how to create empowering mythologies that will evoke courage in deathing and allow for more peace in dying.

Nearing Death Awareness: Discuss the two categories of messages from individuals in the deathing process about death awareness. Compare and contrast the similarities and differences in nearing death awareness and near death experiences.

Healing Grief and Loss: Discuss the three characteristics of appropriate grief work.

NURSING PROCESS

Focus on specifics of assessment, nursing diagnoses, client outcomes, planning, intervention, and evaluation (Table 17–1 and Exhibit 17–1). Instruct students in importance of developing their style of preparation before, during, and at the end of the session.

EXPERIENTIAL EXERCISES

(2 hours. Incorporation of sharing circles (see pp. 7 and 10) and experiential exercises is encouraged for class presentation. Refer to chapter section entitled Specific Interventions for details.)

Planning an Ideal Death: Engage students in exploring the reflective questions about planning an ideal death. This process provides enormous insight about death, myths, beliefs, problem solving, loving, and forgiving.

Learning Forgiveness: Have students review the steps to forgiving self and others. Next provide time for students to write out or share with another student each of these steps in forgiving self and in forgiving another person.

Relaxation and Imagery Scripts for Peace in Deathing and Dying: Provide time for students to experience each of the relaxation and imagery exercises and to share with each other their experiences. These exercises allow us to learn how to open and soften and how to be present in each daily moment, which leads to being in the moment with the deathing and death process.

The Pain Process: Explore how the physical body may be experiencing pain, but the mind's fear of pain is often more intense.

Blending Breaths/Co-meditation: Demonstrate the steps in co-meditation breathing. Have students practice in dyads the co-meditation breathing. Following the experience, encourage the sharing of the co-meditation breathing experience.

Mantras and Prayers. Have students write or choose a mantra or special prayer. Invite students to share their mantra or prayer with the group. Have students share when they used prayer in their own lives or prayed for another or were told by friends or family that they were being prayed for or had been prayed for at certain times, such as during difficult situations.

Reminiscing and Life Review: Ask students to work in dyads and to guide each other using the life review process. Allow time for sharing the experience.

Leavetaking Rituals: Explore the importance of leavetaking rituals and different ways to work through the death of a loved one. Invite students to review certain rituals such as holidays, rearranging and giving away, letting grief be present, sustaining hope and faith, releasing anger and tears, healing memories, and getting unstuck. Invite the sharing of personal stories of working through grief.

Case Study: Have students discuss case studies as well as incorporate a case study in group presentation. Encourage sharing of other client/patient stories focusing on the meaning of the stories, symptoms, illness, and use of specific symbols and metaphors.

ANNOTATED BIBLIOGRAPHY CARDS

Directions for Future Research: Have students choose one or more research questions as an area to explore for annotated bibliography cards. Encourage students to begin collecting articles that can support further investigation.

JOURNAL ENTRIES

Nurse Healer Reflection: Encourage students to use the chapter reflective questions as a guide to journal entries for exploring, understanding, and validating presence and healing.

UNIT IV

LIFESTYLE ALTERATION

Chapter 18

Weight Management: Eating More, Weighing Less

CHAPTER OBJECTIVES

Refer to chapter for specific theory, clinical, and personal objectives. These will provide guidelines for the integration of objectives in class presentation, experiential sessions, and student homework assignments.

CHAPTER OVERVIEW

Obesity is a major health risk and is on the increase. Research studies demonstrate that the best nutrition and food benefits come from a variety of high-fiber, low-fat foods and sensible meal portions. Cognitive strategies, exercise, and stress management interventions are also necessary to maintain an ideal weight.

PROCESS EXERCISE #18

(15-minute opening experiential session using music and at least one raisin per student)

Vision of Healing: Nourishing Wisdom

Often we eat in an unconscious manner. The following exercise is one of mindfulness and being present in the moment as we eat. Give each student a single raisin.

Begin with a guided relaxation exercise (5 minutes) and gradually fade in music of choice. Suggest to students that they can close their eyes or leave their eyes open. If eyes are open ask them to find a spot several feet in front of them to focus on. This allows for a greater ease in following the relaxation and imagery suggestions and reflective experience.

Using techniques for empowering relaxation and imagery scripts (pp. 619–622), gently weave into a guided imagery exercise reflective questions about how the raisin feels within the mouth. As a guide, you will place a raisin in your mouth allowing it to just be. As you experience the raisin taking different moves with increased salivation, as it goes from shriveled to full, you will be guiding the students in exploring the ability to focus on one raisin for 10 minutes or longer.

As the guide you say the following: Place a single raisin on your tongue and just let the raisin be. Do not bite or chew it. It will roll off of your tongue and move around in your mouth with increased salivation. Just notice all parts of your mouth that the raisin touches. After the raisin has swelled (5–10 minutes) to being smooth, gently bite into the raisin, noticing the juice, the meat, and the sweetness of the raisin. Notice the sensation of swallowing the single raisin. What images or memories come? (This raisin exercise can take 10 minutes or longer.) Bring closure to the imagery process.

With soft music still playing, invite students to record in a personal journal (3–5 minutes) any images, process questions and answers, or insight gained. Ask students to bring personal closure to this process. Gradually fade music out. Engage students in a gentle stretching exercise before the theory session begins.

KEY CONCEPTS: THEORY

(1-hour presentation)
OPTIONAL: GUEST SPEAKER(S) AND VIDEO(S)

Guest Speaker(s): Invite a nurse or nutritionist who focuses on nutrition education. Provide guest speaker with the Instructor's Manual suggestions to become familiar with students' assignment before class.

Video(s): Show a video of a practitioner describing and demonstrating one or more holistic modalities in regard to nutrition (rent from media catalog or purchase for school video library). Following the video presentation ask students for their reaction and comments. Discuss video and answer questions.

Definitions: Review definitions and incorporate into presentation.

Raising the Resting Metabolic Rate: Discuss basal metabolic rate, specific dynamic affect, importance of breakfast, and grazing.

Setpoint Theory: Discuss fat thermostat, weight-regulating mechanism, impact of crash dieting, and starvation.

Ultradian Healing Response and Balanced Food Intake: Discuss biologic rhythms, ultradian healing response, and four type of overeaters. Incorporate change theory. (See Chapter 5.)

NURSING PROCESS

Focus on specifics of assessment, nursing diagnoses, client outcomes, planning, intervention, and evaluation (Table 18–1 and Exhibit 18–2). Instruct students in importance of developing their style of preparation before, during, and at the end of the session.

EXPERIENTIAL EXERCISES

(2 hours. Incorporation of sharing circles (see pp. 7 and 10) and experiential exercises is encouraged for class presentation. Refer to chapter section entitled Specific Interventions for details.)

Fat Reduction: Ask students to calculate a personal one full day meal plan including snack foods and determine fat content. Ask students to identify personal steps to achieve or maintain ideal weight (Exhibit 18–1).

Food Guide Pyramid: Have students determine personal steps to achieve a 20% fat diet.

Mood, Hunger, and Eating Satisfaction: Follow guideline questions and have students assess personal moods, hunger, and satisfaction with meals.

Integration of Exercise: Have students assess their current exercise program and use of personal affirmations that are integrated about health, flexibility, strength, and ideal weight while exercising.

Assertion of Bill of Rights: Explore strategies to help students become aware of their rights to help achieve and maintain ideal weight.

Image Change: Discuss strategies to incorporate image change and to reverse negative images that are stored in memory about eating. This is essential for maintaining ideal weight.

Healthy Weight Imagery Scripts: Guide students in imagery scripts that incorporate strategies for enhancing imagery process of being at healthy weight. Scripts include imagining self at ideal weight, affirmations, food guide pyramid, food diary, recognizing hunger, imagining eating at home, eating slowly, eating out, and exercise.

Case Study: Have students discuss case studies as well as incorporate a case study in group presentation. Encourage sharing of other client/patient stories focusing on the meaning of the stories, symptoms, illness, and use of specific symbols and metaphors.

ANNOTATED BIBLIOGRAPHY CARDS

Directions for Future Research: Have students choose one or more research questions as an area to explore for annotated bibliography cards. Encourage students to begin collecting articles that can support further investigation.

JOURNAL ENTRIES

Nurse Healer Reflections: Encourage students to use the chapter reflective questions as a guide to journal entries for exploring, understanding, and validating presence and healing.

Chapter 19

Smoking Cessation: Breathing Free

CHAPTER OBJECTIVES

Refer to chapter for specific theory, clinical, and personal objectives. These will provide guidelines for the integration of objectives in class presentation, experiential sessions, and student homework assignments.

CHAPTER OVERVIEW

Becoming a successful ex-smoker requires commitment to change. For most individuals, this is a step-by-step process. When preparation and healing rituals are incorporated into the change process, the individual has more success with sustained smoking cessation. Cognitive strategies, exercise, and stress management interventions must be explored in order for an individual to become a successful nonsmoker.

PROCESS EXERCISE #19

(15-minute opening experiential session using music and healing objects if desired)

Vision of Healing: Acknowledging Fear

Fear of failure, fear of weight gain, etc., are fears that smokers encounter as they begin the change toward becoming a nonsmoker. Have students experience ordinary fears that surface each day.

Begin with a guided relaxation exercise (5 minutes) and gradually fade in music of choice. Suggest to students that they can close their eyes or leave their eyes open. If eyes are open ask them to find a spot several feet in front of them to focus on. This allows for a greater ease in following the relaxation and imagery suggestions and reflective experience.

Using techniques for empowering relaxation and imagery scripts (pp 619–622), gently weave into a guided imagery exercise reflective questions about different fears such as fear of failure, rejection, unknowns, isolation, dying, loss of control, and so forth. Invite students to bring into their imagery process a specific fear and to reflect on the questions listed. Bring closure to the imagery process.

With soft music still playing, invite students to record in a personal journal (3–5 minutes) any images, process questions and answers, or insight gained. Ask students to bring personal closure to this process. Gradually fade music out. Engage students in a gentle stretching exercise before the theory session begins.

KEY CONCEPTS: THEORY

(1-hour presentation)
OPTIONAL: GUEST SPEAKER(S) AND VIDEO(S)

Guest Speaker(s): Invite one or more nurses who integrate holistic modalities in a smoking cessation program. Provide guest speaker(s) with the Instructor's Manual suggestions to become familiar with students' assignment before class.

Video(s): Show a video of a practitioner describing and demonstrating one or more holistic modalities with smoking cessation (rent from media catalog or purchase for school video library). Following the video presentation ask students for their reaction and comments. Discuss video and answer questions.

Definitions: Review definitions and incorporate into presentation.

Prevalence and Stages for Smoking Cessation: Discuss the eight-stage process for successful smoking cessation. Incorporate change theory. (See Chapter 5.)

Body/Brain/Mind Response: Review physiological and pathophysiological effects of smoking.

Prevention Programs and Strategies: Review research related to successful smoking cessation programs.

NURSING PROCESS

Focus on specifics of assessment, nursing diagnoses, client outcomes, planning, intervention, and evaluation (Table 19–1 and Exhibit 19–2). Instruct students in importance of developing their style of preparation before, during, and at the end of the session.

EXPERIENTIAL EXERCISES

(2 hours. Incorporation of sharing circles (see pp. 7 and 10) and experiential exercises is encouraged for class presentation. Refer to chapter section entitled Specific Interventions for details.)

Smoking Profile: Have students review the smoking profile and complete it if they are smokers (Exhibit 19–1).

Record Habit Breakers: Discuss how smoking is a pervasive, automatic habit. Most smokers need to keep a diary of when, where, how often, and what moods are associated with smoking. See reflective questions listed to help a client record data in a diary. If any students are smokers have them assess where they are in the change process and the next steps to becoming a successful nonsmoker.

Preparation for Quit Date: Reinforce the need for preparation for the quit date. The goal is to be a nonsmoker in 5 days.

Preparation for Nicotine Withdrawal: Discuss the three different strategies for nicotine withdrawal.

Smoke Free Body and Environment: Emphasize the strategies for body detoxification and cleaning of the living environment.

Identification of Habit Breakers: Review strategies to help identify when smoking is most likely to occur and how to create habit breakers to replace negative smoking behaviors.

Integration of Exercise: Integrate exercise as a stress manager and an alternative to smoking. Exercise also is a way to manage weight gain by increasing aerobic activity.

Assertion of Bill of Rights: Explore strategies to help smokers become aware of their rights to be smoke-free.

Integration of Rewards: Explore strategies to create rewards to help a smoker to become smoke-free.

Reinforcement of Positive Self-Talk: Explore strategies to help smokers recognize how interconnected feelings, moods, behaviors, and motivation affect physiology.

Smoking Cessation Imagery Scripts: Integrate strategies for enhancing the imagery process of being smoke-free. Scripts include setting quit date, cleansing body and environment, recognizing smoke signals, and incorporating nutritious eating and exercise.

Case Study: Have students discuss case studies as well as incorporate a case study in group presentation. Encourage sharing of other client/patient stories, focusing on the meaning of the stories, symptoms, illness, and use of specific symbols and metaphors.

ANNOTATED BIBLIOGRAPHY CARDS

Directions for Future Research: Have students choose one or more research questions as an area to explore for annotated bibliography cards. Encourage students to begin collecting articles that can support further investigation.

JOURNAL ENTRIES

Nurse Healer Reflections: Encourage students to use the chapter reflective questions as a guide to journal entries for exploring, understanding, and validating presence and healing.

Chapter 20

Overcoming Addictions: Recovering through Life

CHAPTER OBJECTIVES

Refer to chapter for specific theory, clinical, and personal objectives. These will provide guidelines for the integration of objectives in class presentation, experiential sessions, and student homework assignments.

CHAPTER OVERVIEW

Addiction is literally a disconnection from the human spirit where a person develops a dependence on various aspects of the external world—a substance, a person, a situation, or a behavior. It often leads to a dysfunctional relationship in which the participants are co-dependent. The addicted individual must acknowledge that he or she is not alone in the struggle. In order to overcome an addiction, a person must first admit that the addiction exists. The best chance for recovery occurs when a person has the support of close friends and family, joins a support group, finds a sponsor, and learns habits to change old behaviors.

PROCESS EXERCISE #20

(15-minute opening experiential session using music and healing objects if desired)

Vision of Healing: Changing One's World View

Introduce students to the concept of world view and how at any given time one has a world view. A shift in one's world view is a fundamental and essential step to overcoming an addiction.

Begin with a guided relaxation exercise (5 minutes) and gradually fade in music of choice. Suggest to students that they can close their eyes or leave their eyes open. If eyes are open ask them to find a spot several feet in front of them to focus on. This allows for a greater ease in following the relaxation and imagery suggestions and reflective experience.

Using techniques for empowering relaxation and imagery scripts (pp. 619–622), gently weave into a guided imagery exercise reflective questions about world view and changing world view as given in text. In this script incorporate a world view about daily activities that can be done to care for self and to enhance well-being. Bring closure to the imagery process.

With soft music still playing, invite students to record in a personal journal (3–5 minutes) any images, process questions and answers, or insight gained. Ask students to bring personal closure to this process. Gradually fade music out. Engage students in a gentle stretching exercise before the theory session begins.

KEY CONCEPTS: THEORY

(1-hour presentation)
OPTIONAL: GUEST SPEAKER(S) AND VIDEO(S)

Guest Speaker(s): Invite one or more nurses who integrate holistic modalities in an addiction counseling practice. Provide guest speaker(s) with the Instructor's Manual suggestions to become familiar with students' assignment before class.

Video(s): Show a video of a practitioner describing and demonstrating one or more holistic modalities in a substance abuse program (rent from media catalog or purchase for school video library). Following the video presentation ask students for their reaction and comments. Discuss video and answer questions.

Definitions: Review definitions and incorporate into presentation.

Addiction as an Illness: Discuss how an addiction is literally a disconnection from the human spirit.

Prevalence of Alcoholics and Social Drinkers: Discuss prevalence, deaths, cost, and theories.

Fragmented Families: Discuss how an addiction is a family disease and how a family can break an addiction.

Story Themes of Addictions: Discuss recurring themes: attachment to external resources, poor self-image, anxiety, fear, chaos, pain, and suffering.

Origin of Addiction: Discuss the importance of self-healing around the origin of the trauma leading to an addiction.

Spiritual Development and Transformation: Discuss how spirituality is a process of learning about love, caring, empathy, purpose, and meaning in life. Discuss spiritual transformation as an investigation into one's addiction and the importance of learning new skills to break and sustain change. Incorporate change theory. (See Chapter 5.)

Bodymind Responses: Discuss research supporting the importance of learning new health behaviors in order to break and sustain being free of an addiction.

Ultradian Approach to Addictions: Discuss how substance abusers override their own natural bodymind messenger molecules and the natural ultradian and circadian rest periods with substances. Discuss the ultradian stress response and link this with binges, drugs, and physiologic responses.

NURSING PROCESS

Focus on specifics of assessment, nursing diagnoses, client outcomes, planning, intervention, and evaluation (Table 20–1 and Exhibit 20–2). Instruct students in the importance of developing their style of preparation before, during, and at the end of the session.

EXPERIENTIAL EXERCISES

(2 hours. Incorporation of sharing circles (see pp. 7 and 10) and experiential exercises is encouraged for class presentation. Refer to chapter section entitled Specific Interventions for details.)

Are You a Problem Drinker?: Encourage students to complete this important self-assessment (Exhibit 20–1). If they are concerned about a friend or family member that may have an addiction problem, this tool may be used.

Support from Family and Friends: Encourage students to interview a person who has been part of a family intervention team.

Support Groups and Professional Help: Encourage students to attend a 12-step program for breaking addictions and to discuss with each other their personal response to attending a support meeting. Reinforce the importance of addressing colleague addictions in the workplace and how to be part of a support intervention team.

Learning To Tell a Personal Story: Have students discuss recurrent story themes in 12-step program meetings and how addicted individuals release their attachments to substances, people, situations, or behaviors.

Resistance to Spirituality: Have students identify any spiritual resistance or discomfort that is personally experienced when words such as "in relationship to God," "Higher Power," etc., are used for breaking addictions.

Relaxation and Imagery: Explore how relaxation and imagery skills are strategies to assist the addicted person to access feelings, behaviors, emotions, and to learn how to sustain new health behaviors.

Overcoming Addictions Imagery Scripts: Guide students scripts that incorporate strategies for enhancing relaxation and the imagery process of being addiction-free. Scripts include affirming strengths, overcoming drink/drug signals, AA meeting rehearsal, learning to trust and forgive, and releasing old patterns.

Case Study: Have students discuss case study as well as incorporate a case study in group presentation. Encourage sharing of other client/patient stories, focusing on the meaning of the stories, symptoms, illness, and use of specific symbols and metaphors.

ANNOTATED BIBLIOGRAPHY CARDS

Directions for Future Research: Have students choose one or more research questions as an area to explore for annotated bibliography cards. Encourage students to begin collecting articles that can support further investigation.

JOURNAL ENTRIES

Nurse Healer Reflections: Encourage students to use the chapter reflective questions as a guide to journal entries for exploring, understanding, and validating presence and healing.

UNIT V

HOLISTIC NURSING INTERVENTIONS

Chapter 21

Touch: Connecting with the Healing Power

CHAPTER OBJECTIVES

Refer to chapter for specific theory, clinical, and personal objectives. These will assist with the integration of objectives in class presentation, experiential sessions, and student homework assignments.

CHAPTER OVERVIEW

Many practitioners and recipients of touch modalities report that the end result is more beneficial than the obvious advantageous physical effects. Numerous touch therapies have been developed, are taught, and are practiced by increasing numbers of practitioners. Both direct and indirect body-mind-spirit effects of touch therapies have been demonstrated to enhance healing through one of the body's main sense organs, the skin.

PROCESS EXERCISE #21

(15-minute opening experiential session using music and healing objects if desired)

Vision of Healing: Using Our Healing Hands

Each touch therapy has specific touch skills. Some of these skills are stroking, kneading, manipulating, light touch, pressure point, and working within an energy field.

Begin with a guided relaxation exercise (5 minutes) and gradually fade in music of choice. Suggest to students that they can close their eyes or leave them open. If eyes are left open ask them to find a spot several feet in front of them to focus on. This allows for a greater ease in following the suggestions and reflective experience.

Using techniques for empowering relaxation and imagery scripts (pp. 619–622), gently weave into a guided imagery exercise reflective questions as follows: What does touch mean to you? How do you feel when you touch an elderly person, a terminally ill child, or someone who seeks stress reduction? Add three to five more reflective questions in regard to touch. Bring closure to the imagery process.

With soft music still playing, invite students to record in a personal journal (3–5 minutes) any images, process questions and answers, or insight gained. Ask students to bring personal closure to this process. Gradually fade music out. Engage students in a gentle stretching exercise before the theory session begins.

KEY CONCEPTS: THEORY

(1-hour presentation)
OPTIONAL: GUEST SPEAKER(S) AND VIDEO(S)

Guest Speaker(s): Invite one or more nurses experienced in touch therapies. Provide guest speaker(s) with the Instructor's Manual suggestions to become familiar with students' reading assignment before class.

Video(s): Show a video of a practitioner who describes, demonstrates, and integrates one or more touch modalities (rent from media catalog or purchase for school video library). Following the video presentation ask students for their reaction and comments. Discuss video and answer questions.

Definitions: Review definitions and incorporate into presentation.

Touch in Ancient Times: Review the multi-thousand-year history of touch. Discuss how massage was used with dream work to prepare individuals for healing during the height of Greek civilization.

Cultural Variations: Attitudes toward touch vary from culture to culture and from one individual to another. Encourage students to be sensitive to individual differences and diverse cultural attitudes, such as touch as taboo in one culture versus touch as health enhancing in another culture.

Validating Studies: Review clinical research to support the effectiveness of touch therapies in a variety of health care delivery settings.

Touch Techniques: Explore how touch is a method of bodymind communication. Discuss the basic techniques of therapeutic massage, therapeutic touch, healing touch, acupressure, shiatzu, and reflexology.

NURSING PROCESS

Focus on specifics of assessment, nursing diagnoses, client outcomes, planning, intervention, and evaluation (Table 21–1 and Exhibit 21–1). Instruct students in the importance of developing their style of preparation before, during, and at the end of the session.

EXPERIENTIAL EXERCISES

(2 hours. Incorporation of sharing circles (see pp. 7 and 10) and experiential exercises is encouraged for class presentation. Refer to chapter section entitled Specific Interventions for details.)

Touch: Have students work in dyads and begin the touch experiences. Throughout the exercise have the students briefly share their bodymind sensations with their practice partner. Guide the students through the basic therapeutic massage strokes as they apply them to their partner's back. Begin the experience by leading both the giver and the receiver of touch through a series of relaxation steps. For an advanced session add music and imagery to the exercise.

Basic Swedish Massage Strokes: This massage modality is the one used historically in nursing practice. It is most useful for complete bodymind relaxation to evoke sleep, to reduce stress, or as stimulating therapy to increase circulation in the bedridden patient.

Effleurage (ef-flur-ahj): A French word meaning to touch lightly. Use this stroke to begin and end the session. This light touch acquaints the recipient with the touch of the practitioner and warms up the area for later strokes. Instruct the student practitioner to run his or her hands along the length of the torso from the neck to the base of the recipient's spine or from the base of the spine up to the base of the neck. Practice using the stroke with the joined tips of the fingers, the palms of the hands, and the ball of the thumb. The increased circulation and increased sweat gland activity creates waste products movement from inner cellular storage into the blood stream and out of their body. Feel the rejuvenation of the dermal and epidermal layers of your skin.

Petrissage (pet-ris-ahj): Student practitioner, with one or both hands, carefully lift up the recipient's muscles along each vertical side of the back, then roll, wring, and squeeze them. Ask the recipient to feel the increasing circulation and to imagine lactic acid moving out of the cells and the passage of nutrients to the cells, contributing to increasing muscle size and strength.

Friction: Student practitioner, using thumb or fingertips, apply deep, circular movement near the joints and other body areas such as the sides of the spine. Recipient, feel the release of knots that occur when muscle fibers bind together. Become aware that this decrease in muscle tension allows for more flexible joints, tendons, and muscles.

Tapotement (tap-ot-mon): Student practitioner, use this short, chopping movement to chop or hack with the edge of your hand on the recipient. Tap with your fingertips, and clap with the palms or the flat surface of your hands and fingers. For a few seconds apply extra stimulation if the recipient has muscle strains or spasms.

Vibration or shaking: Student practitioner, spread your hands or fingers on the recipient's back, press down firmly, and rapidly shake for a few seconds with a trembling motion. Recipient, feel this stroke stimulating your nervous system and increasing the power of the muscles to contract. Focus on how these techniques boost circulation and increase the activities of the glands.

At the end of the session ask the students to exchange impressions about the perceived length of the session, the effectiveness of the exercise, the physical effort on the part of the practitioner, and the degree of relaxation on the part of the recipient. If time permits, ask the partners to switch roles and repeat the steps in this exercise.

Case Study: Have students discuss case studies as well as incorporate a case study in group presentation. Encourage students to share other client/patient stories and to focus on the meaning of the symptoms, disease, illness, and use of specific symbols and metaphors.

ANNOTATED BIBLIOGRAPHY CARDS

Directions for Future Research: Have students choose one or more research questions as an area to explore for annotated bibliography cards. Encourage students to begin collecting articles that can support further investigation.

JOURNAL ENTRIES

Nurse Healer Reflections: Encourage students to use the chapter reflective questions as a guide to journal entries for exploring, understanding, and validating presence and healing.

Chapter 22

Relaxation: Opening the Door to Change

CHAPTER OBJECTIVES

Refer to chapter for specific theory, clinical, and personal objectives. These will assist with the integration of objectives in class presentation, experiential sessions, and student homework assignments.

CHAPTER OVERVIEW

Relaxation calms the bodymind and helps us to focus inward. Regardless of the approach used, the end result is a movement of a person toward balance and healing. Relaxation exercises can be taught under almost any circumstances. These interventions not only can reduce fear and anxiety associated with medical and nursing procedures, but, once learned, may also be used in all aspects of a client's life.

PROCESS EXERCISE #22

(15-minute opening experiential session using music and healing objects if desired)

Vision of Healing: Creating Receptive Quiet

Learning to create a state of mindfulness where there is an absence of physical, mental, and emotional tension is an important healing modality. As the skills of being in the present moment are cultivated, we have greater opportunities toward wholeness and well-being.

Begin with a guided relaxation exercise (5 minutes) and gradually fade in music of choice. Suggest to students that they can close their eyes or leave their eyes open. If eyes are open ask them to find a spot several feet in front of them to focus on. This allows for a greater ease in following the relaxation and imagery suggestions and reflective experience.

Using techniques for empowering relaxation and imagery scripts (pp. 619–622), gently weave into a guided imagery exercise reflective questions as the power of the healing rhythm of relaxed breathing is explored. Bring closure to the imagery process.

With soft music still playing, invite students to record in a personal journal (3–5 minutes) any images, process questions and answers, or insight gained. Ask students to bring personal closure to this process. Gradually fade music out. Engage students in an easy stretching exercise before the theory session begins.

KEY CONCEPTS: THEORY

(1-hour presentation)
OPTIONAL: GUEST SPEAKER(S) AND VIDEO(S)

Guest Speaker(s): Invite a nurse or professional who uses biofeedback to demonstrate biofeedback procedure. Give students an opportunity to use the biofeedback equipment and to incorporate relaxation and imagery techniques while using the equipment. Provide the guest speaker with Instructor's Manual suggestions to become familiar with students' assignment before class.

Video(s): Show a video that demonstrates use of relaxation, self-hypnosis, or biofeedback (rent from a media catalog or purchase for school library). Following the video presentation ask students for their reaction and comments. Discuss video and answer questions.

Definitions: Review definitions and incorporate into presentation.

Relaxation: Discuss general definition and the psychophysiologic changes that accompany relaxation. Review specific strategies of meditation, progressive relaxation, autogenics, hypnosis and self-hypnosis, biofeedback, open focus, and relaxation response. Compare and contrast these different relaxation strategies. Discuss their clinical application in various clinical settings.

Relaxation Commonalities: Explore the relaxation commonalties of mindfulness, time, timelessness, passive volition, and compassionate guidance.

Relaxation Caveats: Discuss the relaxation caveats of control, lack of time, choices, medications, body scans, and cueing.

NURSING PROCESS

Focus on specifics of assessment, nursing diagnoses, client outcomes, planning, intervention, and evaluation (Table 22–1 and Exhibit 22–1). Instruct students in importance of developing their style of preparation before, during, and at the end of the session.

EXPERIENTIAL EXERCISES

(2 hours. Incorporation of sharing circles (see pp. 7 and 10) and experiential exercises is encouraged in class presentation. Refer to chapter section Specific Interventions for details.)

Relaxation Interventions: Prior to this class ask students to pick one or a combination of breathing techniques and apply them to the stressful moments for one week. Have students share new skills about their increased awareness of where tension accumulates in their body during stressful moments.

Have students work in dyads and guide each other in general breathing exercises, progressive muscle relaxation, autogenic training, open focus, and the relaxation response. Discuss the experience of being a guide and being the recipient of relaxation strategies and what worked best and least while being guided in each intervention.

Meditation: Explore difference in relaxation and meditation. Ask students to sit for a 20-minute period. Share how quieting the mind is a challenge and requires more discipline to enter into deep meditative states.

Prayer: Encourage students to write or read a short prayer and to focus on the inward experience of moving into a contemplative state of being. Explore the faith factor that occurs with relaxation, particularly when individuals choose their own prayer.

Biofeedback: If a guest speaker is not part of the class, visit a biofeedback laboratory. Provide the students with an opportunity to use the biofeedback equipment in order to experience constant feedback of various degrees of relaxation. Have each student identify a commonly used piece of equipment in nursing practice, and describe how it could be used as a biofeedback device.

Hypnosis and Self-Hypnosis: Investigate the differences in hypnosis and self-hypnosis. Ask students to recognize negative self-talk and to create a healthier self-talk dialogue. Have students share a clinical situation where they assisted a client to identify negative self-talk and then helped the client construct a healthier self-talk.

Case Study: Have students discuss case studies involving the combined interventions (Figures 22–2 and 22–3) as well as incorporate a case study in group presentation. Encourage students to share other client/patient stories and to focus on the meaning of symptoms, disease, illness, and use of specific symbols and metaphors.

ANNOTATED BIBLIOGRAPHY CARDS

Directions for Future Research: Have students choose one or more research questions as an area to explore for annotated bibliography cards. Encourage students to begin collecting articles that can support further investigation.

JOURNAL ENTRIES

Nurse Healer Reflections: Encourage students to use the chapter reflective questions as a guide to journal entries for exploring, understanding, and validating presence and healing.

Chapter 23

Imagery: Awakening the Inner Healer

CHAPTER OBJECTIVES

Refer to chapter for specific theory, clinical, and personal objectives. These will provide guidelines for the integration of objectives in class presentation, experiential sessions, and student homework assignments.

CHAPTER OVERVIEW

Imagery is the most ancient and potent healing resource in the history of medicine. Through our senses, imagery creates the interface between body, mind, and spirit. It is like a midwife, assisting the birth of conscious expression from the depths of inner experience.

PROCESS EXERCISE #23

(15-minute opening experiential session using music and other healing objects if desired)

Vision of Healing: Modeling a Wellness Lifestyle

Self-assessment is an essential step in modeling a wellness lifestyle. Ask students to reflect on their Self-Assessments and the Circle of Human Potential (Chapter 9).

Begin with a guided relaxation exercise (5 minutes) and gradually fade in music of choice. Suggest to students that they can close their eyes or leave their eyes open. If eyes are open ask them to find a spot several feet in front of them to focus on. This allows for a greater ease in following the relaxation and imagery suggestions and reflective experience.

Using techniques for empowering relaxation and imagery scripts (pp. 619–622), gently weave into a guided imagery exercise reflective questions about where they are in their life at this time. Have them reflect on the areas of self-assessment, any desired change, and what it would take to change attitudes, beliefs, and support systems. Ask students to go forward in time to the year 2000 and to experience in their imagination modeling and living the circle of human potential as you slowly integrate imagery suggestions about each area. Bring closure to the imagery process.

With soft music still playing, invite students to record in a personal journal (3–5 minutes) any images, process questions and answers, or insight gained. Ask students to bring personal closure to this process. Gradually fade music out. Engage students in a gentle stretching exercise before the theory session begins.

KEY CONCEPTS: THEORY

(1-hour presentation)
OPTIONAL: GUEST SPEAKER(S) AND VIDEO(S)

Guest Speaker(s): Invite one or more nurses experienced in the use of imagery in clinical practice or an art therapist. Provide guest speaker(s) with the Instructor's Manual suggestions to become familiar with students' assignment before class.

Video(s): Show a video of a practitioner describing and demonstrating one or more imagery modalities in clinical practice (rent from media catalog or purchase for school video library). Following video presentation ask students for their reaction and comments. Discuss video and answer questions.

Definitions: Review definitions and incorporate into presentation.

Effects of Imagery on Physiology and the Senses: Increase the students' awareness of the senses. Become aware of how each sense, when stimulated, can enhance another sense. Incorporation of experiential imagery exercise with theory is very effective. Refer to experiential exercises.

Imagery and State-Dependent Learning: Discuss the concept of state-dependent learning and memory. (Refer to Chapter 4 exercises.)

Imagery Theories: Review the three theories discussed. Use the example of a worry or a fear (test anxiety, money, relationships, time, complications of surgery, etc.) as each theory is analyzed to demonstrate how an individual can create a new healing image in self-dialogue and imagery rehearsal. Connect theories with different types of imagery in an experiential session.

Types of Imagery: Discuss the 9 types of imagery, reinforcing that we use one or more of the senses in all of these imagery patterns. See examples in experiential section.

Imagery with Disease: Refer to bone, wound, burn graft, and immune illustrations for examples (Figure 23–1 to 23–4). Reinforce that all client/patient teaching and learning sessions engage the imagination. As nurses teach clients/patients imagery skills of how to identify their dominant sensory modality, their desired outcomes, the normal physiologic healing process and external healing resources, and their internal healing resources, the teaching/learning sessions become much more effective. The student and the client/patient are actively involved in the process because both hemispheres are engaged.

Concrete Objective Information: Discuss the subjective and objective experiences that clients/patients are faced with during tests and procedures. Review documented subjective experience descriptors during stressful events (Table 23–1). Have students add to this list.

Techniques for Empowering Imagery Scripts and Spoken Words: Discuss truism, embedded command, linkage, reframing, metaphor, therapeutic double-bind, synesthesia, and interspersal. These techniques can make a better guide and enhance the effectiveness of the healing script. Have students increase their awareness of these techniques in teaching sessions.

NURSING PROCESS

Focus on specifics of assessment, client outcomes, planning, intervention, and evaluation (Table 23–2 and Exhibit 23–1). Instruct students in the importance of developing their style of preparation before, during, and at the end of the session.

EXPERIENTIAL EXERCISES

(2 hours. Incorporation of sharing circles (see pp. 7 and 10) and experiential exercises is encouraged in class presentation. Refer to chapter section entitled Specific Interventions for details.)

Guided Imagery. Coach students in how to guide others in a general imagery exercise. Throughout the course have students briefly share experiences and personal dominant sensory modalities with different exercises. With eyes closed ask students to experience:

Touch: Place place hands on lap and feel texture of clothing on skin. What images or memories come?

Sound: Sound a chime or bell. What images or memories come?

Sight: Focus on a special color in the mind's eye. What images or memories come?

Smell: Pass a cotton pad with vanilla on it. Let each student smell the fragrance. What images or memories come from the smell of vanilla?

Taste: Imagine a lemon. Feel its texture. Now cut and smell the lemon. Imagine a drop of lemon juice on the tongue. Notice increased salivation. Just thinking about this experience produced what kind of imagery sensations? What images or memories come?

Movement: What inner experiences occurred with stimulation of the other senses? What images or memories come?

Guide students or coach students in how to guide a relaxation and imagery exercise to identify the different types of imagery. Music will enhance the awareness of the different senses as well as the imagery process.

Receptive Imagery : Identify where tension is carried in the body. What are your first body sensations or inner awareness of tension being present? Discover your dominant sensory modality (see text for details).

Active Imagery: Take the receptive image of tension and begin to create or change it to a helpful, healing image/sensation.

Correct Biologic Imagery: If any current health problem exists, identify images from textbooks, magazines, or drug ads that incorporate physiology to better understand the physiologic healing process. Review bone, wound, and burn graft healing images.

Symbolic Imagery: Remember symbolic images emerge from the psyche to evoke healing. These images are one's own hero's journey and personal mythology. These images are influenced by media, art, cartoons, symbols, and fantasy characters. For example, symbolic images may reflect deep-seated past trauma as well as current discomfort that may also be associated with physical injury or dysfunction. For example, for neck pain, symbolic images may be knots, knives, pitchforks, and so forth. The healing images would involve the release, removal, untying, melting, or whatever seems to work given the nature of the symbolic image. The shift from correct biologic image to symbolic image usually is a dramatic event and often involves one or more of the senses.

Process Imagery: Have students identify a current situation (physical, relationship, spiritual) that is in need of healing and rehearse step-by-step images directed toward the outcomes desired.

End-State Imagery: Take the process imagery just identified and imagine it in a final, healed state or rehearse the final outcome desired.

General Healing Imagery: Identify a healing image, color, sound, etc., that has qualities that evoke healing and inner peace.

Images in Client/Patient Education: Encourage students to begin a file of helpful images to use in client/patient education. You may wish to have each student choose one disease/illness and present a teaching session to a class throughout the course.

Facilitation and Interpretation of the Imagery Process: Encourage students in the daily journaling process to record their own images of stress symptoms and the personal meaning of these symptoms. Share different client/patient images and how the client/patient interpreted the symptoms, worries, or fears. To elicit these images encourage the student to use the technique for empowering the spoken word. Refer to the guidelines for teaching the imagery process of identifying the problem/disease, the inner healing resources, and the external healing resources.

Guided Imagery Scripts: Have students work in dyads in class or out of class using one or more of the specific scripts. Encourage students to share with each other what part of the guiding worked best and what could have been more effective. Follow the guidelines for imagery scripts to enhance the use of imagery as a nursing intervention. Have student use same interventions with family members or friends to gain more experience.

Drawing: Reinforce that the drawing exercise is to gain access to internal information of which an individual is not normally aware. Drawing helps the individual to connect with inner healing resources, creativity, and problem solving. It has nothing to do with one's drawing ability. Using crayons, colored markers, oil pastels, and paper, follow the suggestions given in the textbook for group drawing.

Disease/Symptom Drawing: Have students work with a family member, friend, or client/patient who has symptoms/disease. Review symbolism, colors, and associations to better understand the imagery process (Tables 23-3, 23-4, and 23-5). Follow the guidelines given on helping the individual identify the disease or disability, the internal healing resources, and the external healing resources. Explore the vividness and strength of the internal and external healing resources to eliminate, reverse, or stabilize the symptoms/disease and move the individual toward desired outcomes.

Group Drawing: Have students follow the guidelines for group drawing, identifying all the things for which they are thankful or that excite them about life. As each student is given the opportunity to share a personal story, reinforce the healing moment and presence of being listened to by another and how in the listening and the telling of a story healing occurs.

Drawing a Mandala: Follow the guidelines given for mandalas. Encourage students to buy a special notebook and special pens, oil pastels, or crayons and to do a series of mandalas. Place a date on each one with a few words recording certain life events, either current or past. Have students share these, particularly when deep insight has been gained.

Case Study: Have students discuss case studies as well as incorporate a case study in group presentation. Encourage sharing of other client/patient stories, focusing on the meaning of the symptoms, disease, illness, and use of specific symbols and metaphors.

ANNOTATED BIBIOGRAPHY CARDS

Directions for Future Research: Have students choose one or more research questions as an area to explore for annotated bibliography cards. Encourage students to begin collecting articles that can support further investigation.

JOURNAL ENTRIES

Nurse Healer Reflections: Encourage students to use the chapter reflective questions as a guide to journal entries for exploring, understanding, and validating presence and healing.

Chapter 24

Music Therapy: Hearing the Melody of the Soul

CHAPTER OBJECTIVES

Refer to chapter for specific theory, clinical, and personal objectives. These will assist with the integration of objectives in class presentation, experiential sessions, and student homework assignments.

CHAPTER OVERVIEW

Music has been a vital part of all societies and cultures, no matter how primitive or advanced. It is of no surprise then that music is currently being applied as an alternative therapy in health care. Music therapy is a behavioral science that is concerned with the use of specific kinds of music to effect changes in behavior, emotions, and physiology. As nurses incorporate music therapy into all areas of clinical practice they can reduce the psychophysiologic stress, anxiety, and pain of clients/patients as well as in their personal lives.

PROCESS EXERCISE #22

(15-minute opening experiential session using music and healing objects if desired)

Vision of Healing: Composing the Harmony

There is something about the power of music that cannot be expressed in verbal language. Music literally can flow into every cell in the body when one is in a relaxed state.

Begin with a guided relaxation exercise (5 minutes) and gradually fade in music of choice. Suggest to students that they can close their eyes or leave their eyes open. If eyes are open ask them to find a spot several feet in front of them to focus on. This allows for a greater ease in following the relaxation and imagery suggestions and reflective experience.

Using techniques for empowering relaxation and imagery scripts (pp. 619–622), gently weave into a guided music exercise reflective questions from the music script Merging the Bodymind with Music. Bring closure to the guided music therapy process.

With soft music still playing, invite students to record in a personal journal (3–5 minutes) any images, process questions and answers, or insight gained. Ask students to bring personal closure to this process. Gradually fade music out. Engage students in an easy stretching exercise before the theory session is begun.

KEY CONCEPTS: THEORY

(1-hour presentation)
OPTIONAL: GUEST SPEAKER(S) AND VIDEO(S)

Guest Speaker(s): Invite a nurse who uses music in clinical practice or a music therapist. Provide the guest speaker(s) with the Instructor's Manual suggestions to become familiar with the students' assignment before class.

Video(s): Show a video that demonstrates use of music for relaxation or during painful medical or surgical procedures (rent from a media catalog or purchase for school library). Following the video presentation ask students for their reaction and comments. Discuss video and answer questions.

Definitions: Review definitions and incorporate into presentation.

Music Theory and Research: Review the music from a historical perspective.

Origin of Sound: Discuss the principles and theories of sound to understand fully its tremendous capacity to achieve therapeutic psychophysiologic outcomes.

Purpose of Music Therapy: Discuss the purpose of music and its application in the clinical setting.

Shifting States of Consciousness: Discuss nonordinary levels of consciousness that occur with music. Review experiential time and the components of tension and resolution.

Psychophysiologic Responses: Explore the effects of music therapy on hemispheric functioning, the limbic system, human bodies, imagery, emotions, and the senses.

Music Therapy Application: Review the various outcomes that can be achieved with music therapy.

Music Therapy in Clinical Settings: Share the different clinical settings where music has been used as a healing intervention.

Selection of Appropriate Music: Explore importance of music selection, New Age music, hospital music, individual preference, the iso-principle, and how to record a personal tape.

NURSING PROCESS

Focus on specifics of assessment, nursing diagnoses, client outcomes, planning, intervention, and evaluation (Table 24–1 and Exhibit 24–1). Instruct students in the importance of developing their style of preparation before, during, and at the end of the session.

EXPERIENTIAL EXERCISES

(2 hours. Incorporation of sharing circles (see pp. 7 and 10) and experiential exercises is encouraged in class presentation. Refer to chapter section Specific Interventions for details.)

Development of an Audio/Video Cassette Library: Have students develop an audio/video library for use throughout the semester. Follow the guidelines for a check-in and check-out procedure.

Music Therapy Scripts: Incorporate the music scripts provided in the chapter. Allow time for students to share their experiences with each other. At the end of the session provide students with paper, crayons, and colored markers for a drawing session.

Case Study: Have students discuss case studies involving the combined interventions as well as incorporate a case study in group presentation. Encourage students to share other client/patient stories and to focus on the meaning of symptoms, disease, illness, and use of specific symbols and metaphors.

ANNOTATED BIBLIOGRAPHY CARDS

Directions for Future Research: Have students choose one or more research questions as an area to explore for annotated bibliography cards. Encourage students to begin collecting articles that can support further investigation.

JOURNAL ENTRIES

Nurse Healer Reflections: Encourage students to use the chapter reflective questions as a guide to journal entries for exploring, understanding, and validating presence and healing.

Appendix A

Guidelines for Creating a Healing Tapestry

There are many unique learning opportunities and modalities for your students and even experienced practicing nurses to deepen their understanding of presence and healing. We have adapted the American Town Hall Wall* concept and call the process/experiential exercise "Creating a Healing Tapestry." The size of the healing tapestry is determined by class size. You can have several small or several large blank tapestries, depending on your preference. It can be as simple as using large pieces of brown wrapping paper or a small or large blanket to which pieces of paper can be taped or pinned. However, we encourage a special blank tapestry be created. Felt, for instance, is an ideal material to work with.

A tapestry created for use with 48 students is shown in Figure 3. The tapestry background is made of light purple felt and framed with a 3" black felt border. It is divided into 48 8½" × 11" squares which are separatd by 2" black felt strips.

The 88" × 2" dimensions of the finished tapestry, which accommodate 8 squares across and 5 down, was arrived at with the following addition:

68" (8 8 1/2" squares across)	66" (6 11" squares down)
6" (2 3" -black felt side borders)	6" (2 3"-black felt bottom/top borders)
<u>14"</u> (7 2"-black felt dividing strips	<u>10"</u> (5 2"-black felt dividing strips)
88" across the top of the tapestry	82" from top to bottom of the tapestry

Felt comes in a variety of widths, all smaller than the needed dimensions of the background. It will be necessary to have at least one seam attaching two strips of the felt, which can then be cut to the 88" × 82" size.

Students can be given standard-size (8½" × 11"), light-colored construction paper and black, large felt-tip markers, pens, and/or crayons with which to

---

* The authors wish to thank Beverly Dunaway and Sustainable Strategies, Tiburon, California, for the introduction to the American Town Hall Wall and assistance with photographs. For more information on the Town Hall Wall write: Phyllis Yampolsky, PY and Associates, 888 Manhattan Avenue, Brooklyn, NY 11222.

create their statements/expressions/drawings. A more elaborate exercise is for each student to select a small square of felt and create a pattern from a variety of colored yarns that are attached to the felt with glue. Their paper or felts squares can be affixed to the tapestry by sticking adhesive-backed male velcro dots to the back of the paper, which then easily adheres to an open square on the felt tapestry.

It might be a good idea to create a number of statements/expressions/drawings of your own to add to blank paper squares or design yarn patterns to felt squares to complete the tapestry should you have a number slightly less than appropriate for a finished tapestry.

Introduce students to the healing process as follows:

Healing is a lifelong journey into understanding the wholeness of human existence. Along this journey, our lives mesh with clients, families, and colleagues, where moments of new meaning and insight emerge in the midst of crisis. Healing occurs when we help clients, families, others, and ourselves embrace what is feared most. It occurs when we seek harmony and balance. Healing is learning how to open what has been closed so that we can expand our inner potentials. It is the fullest expression of oneself that is demonstrated by the light and shadow and the male and female principles that reside within each of us. It is accessing what we have forgotten about connections, unity, and interdependence. With a new awareness of these interrelationships, healing becomes possible, and the experiences of nurse healers become actualized. A *nurse healer* is one who facilitates another person's growth toward wholeness (body-mind-spirit) or who assists another with stabilization of a disease process, recovery from illness, or transition to peaceful death.

Next, invite students to write different qualities of healing and healing moments, symbols, etc., on colored construction paper or to create a small healing tapestry with felt and yarns. In a quiet, reflective manner as music continues to play softly, ask students to attach their contribution to the blank tapestry, thus completing the healing tapestry. Allow time for group sharing.

There are many adaptations of this experience as seen in Figure 5. Invite students to think of different word combinations as follows:

Joy: Invite joy, embrace joy, live joy, dance with joy, see joy in a cloud, share joy, and embody joy.

Wisdom: See you are wise, cherish wisdom, speak the truth, be fully present, listen with the heart, forgive ignorance, spread the light.

Lovingkindness: Trust love, let go of fear, let go of despair, love life, let go of anger, love the sacred, love who you are.

Healing: Heal thyself, heal family, heal the earth, heal with forgiveness, heal with love, heal with laughter, and heal with faith.

Appendix B

Script: Creating a Healing Taspestry

INTRODUCTION: A tapestry of healing allows us to reflect on the dynamics of healing. Each of you will create a small tapestry that will be placed with other creations onto the blank tapestry. There is no right or wrong way. Just allow your images to come during a guided relaxation and imagery experience.

DIRECTIONS: This script is written as if students will be applying colored yarns to a small colored square of felt. Colored construction paper, crayons, or colored markers may also be used. To attach the student's piece to the tapestry, a small adhesive-backed male velcro dot will be attached to the back of the felt after the piece is completed. Invite students to find a comfortable place to sit or lie down as the guided relaxation and imagery exercise begins accompanied by music to enhance the process prior to the actual creating of their piece.

SCRIPT: As your mind becomes clearer and clearer, feel it becoming more and more alert. Somewhere deep inside of you... a light begins to glow. Sense this happening... the light growing brighter and more intense... This is your body-mind-spirit communication center. Breath into it... energize it with your breath. The light is powerful and penetrating... and a beam begins to grow out of it to guide you in creating your small unique tapestry that will become part of a large group healing tapestry.

    Imagine that you are beginning a small tapestry to contribute to a group healing tapestry. Create a healing space where you will do your sacred work. Right now, focus on your beautiful blank felt that will become part of the group tapestry... and what are the colors that appeal to the artist who resides within you.

    In front of you are exquisite threads of many colors, textures, and shimmering metallics... Choose the threads to represent your healing... a beautiful thread to represent each of your healing potentials... your joy, peace, harmony, kindness, presence... your courage, truth, patience... your love, honor, trust... your fears, strengths, weaknesses... your light and shadow... your clarity, humor, abundance... your memories, magical places, compassion, forgiveness... your wisdom, purpose, meaning...

And selecting additional threads to represent releasing, opening, seeking, touching, caring, remembering, expressing, responding... more threads for affirming, changing, creating, intending... for sensing, planning, quieting, attuning... threads for softening, forgiving, clearing... for awakening, journeying, transcending, attending... threads for receiving, presencing, listening, doing... for being, enlivening, engaging... for letting go, entering the void...

More threads to represent healing of family, friends, colleagues... for community, global nations, and relations... for all things living and nonliving... for healing moments, hurting moments... spinning your healing threads of light from your healing core... your healing source of beingness...

And now you are beginning to join each thread with your intrinsic rhythm... Sit for a while.... with rhythmic breathing... Let the designs, colors and movements of a spirit-filled tapestry begin to form... And let your rhythms of healing spirit begin to dance. You are aware of becoming at one with the work, to serve the work and the moment... feeling the energy of many higher beings surrounding you... your soul expanding upward and outward... penetrating all of your energy systems... acknowledging what part of you is in need of healing... honoring the challenges before you... asking for new understanding in this healing process... receiving the inner wisdom... and new ways to connect with your higher self...

If it seems right... choose some healing objects to incorporate into your tapestry. As you choose these objects... let the sacredness of each object speak to you... such as stones, flowers, seashells, medallions, beads, grasses... representing you, people and things which are sacred... who may be in need of being remembered or in need of healing.

Focusing now on the patterns and designs... the squares, circles, mosaics, or others images... that will flow into your healing tapestry. The time has come to begin the next phase...

You feel the energy rising forth to begin the intermeshing, connecting, and coming together of the beautiful threads... begin now to push and pull with the rhythm of creating... adding sacred objects... breathing and feeling your intrinsic balance... journeying deep into your soul... tapping your inner wisdom, knowledge, and answers...

You are now placing the final threads into the tapestry... feel the energy... placing the final sacred objects in and on the tapestry...

the work has reached a stopping point for now... The energy fields... the weaving technology... your mind... your spirit... embracing the dynamic dance of flowing... connecting... intertwining... synchronizing... There seems to be an endless exchange of body-mind-spirit elements of living and nonliving... happening without trying... releasing into... letting it happen... the rhythm of your hands weaving in and out... threads blending... in and out...

Just notice... being fully present in the moment... allowing the healing currents to resonate in every cell of your beingness... new visions of healing emerging... inspirations coming...

Sit with your healing tapestry... What patterns have emerged? What emotions do you feel? What kind of energy is present for you? What about you is still in need of healing? What can you do to bring about that healing? Do you feel a connection with your work? Do you feel open to the inner wisdom gained from this process? What are the notes and melody of your healing song? What truths resonate within you... coming from your inner resonating healing core?

Take a few energizing breaths... and as you come back into full awareness of the healing space within you... as you sit in your healing room... know that whatever is right for you at this point in time is unfolding... just as it should... and that you have done your best, regardless of the outcome.

CLOSURE: With music still playing invite students to continue the experience of sacred work as they attach their individual tapestry creations to the large blank tapestry. Suggest the following:

With an awareness of a sense of sacredness, let yourself now attach your sacred creation onto the large blank tapestry with all the others. Feel the experience as you view the work of others with your own... breathing deeply with each inbreath... with each outbreath... an opportunity to release more... to feel gratitude and healing... for contributing to a master tapestry... for every thread you have touched... for every person and living and nonliving thing you have remembered... the extending into and facilitating of the healing process.

And now... hear yourself sharing your healing work and the experience of contributing to a group tapestry with your colleagues... with others... being open... letting yourself be vulnerable... not judging... present in the moment... telling about your tapestry creation... sharing parts of your healing journey...

Guidelines for Mindfulness Practice

What a wonderful opportunity to learn how to be present in the moment with our body, mind, and spirit. Healing happens in the present moment, not in the past or in the future. As we set aside time each day to practice mindfulness, we learn to recognize essential steps for healing. These are such qualities as softening, opening, receiving, forgiving, empathy, compassion, truth, and lovingkindness. There are many ways to begin your practice. You might use strategies such as relaxation, imagery, music, prayer, meditation, movement, or walking meditation. Some guidelines for beginning a practice of mindfulness are:

- Set aside time each day to develop a practice of sitting mindfully for a minimun of 10 minutes each day.
- Find a quiet place and a comfortable place to practice.
- If your mind wanders and begins to attend to things that need to be done, places to go, unfinished business or conversations with self or others, bring your mind back to the present moment. Some ways to do this are to focus on the breath, just noticing the breath in and the breath out. You may wish to see each thought as it comes. In your mind, place each thought on a leaf and see it flowing away in a stream of water. (Refer to Chapter 22 for more details on relaxation and mindfulness practice.)

You might find that you get bored with practice, cut it short, get uncomfortable, get angry, dislike certain emotions, or decide that nothing is happening. These are all natural events as we learn to quiet the constant mind chatter or self-talk. Just approach your practice with a sense of exploring, opening, and lightening to the experience of being in the moment. Let go of any competitiveness or thinking there is a right way. If any uncomfortable emotions or memories come forward, you can either be with them for new insight or take a deep breath, open your eyes, and these experiences will leave. If you wish to delve into these uncomfortable emotions and feel stuck, you may wish to seek professional assistance from a nurse therapist or a counselor who specializes in certain areas (e.g., self-esteem, abuse work, loss/grief work, etc.).

As we learn to be in the moment, we access our natural wisdom. This occurs because we begin to notice the nature of our body, mind, and spirit when we create a state of intention, presence, and recognize new understanding, and inner peace.

Guidelines for Journaling

Journaling is a special process of recording events, thoughts, feelings, dreams, fears, losses, trauma/wounds, healing moments, and inner and external healing resources. There is not a correct or right way to journal. You may find that your journaling may go from structured to free-form with no structure. Read Chapter 14 on structured and unstructured journals. This chapter also helps you gain a deeper understanding of the journaling process and self-reflection.

You can write on loose pieces of blank or lined paper and keep these pages in a folder. However, when you choose a special notebook and writing pen or colored markers to record words and images, the process seems to take on a deeper significance. A few suggestions are offered:

- Set aside a minimum of 5 minutes a day to write in your journal outside of class.
- Find a quiet, comfortable place to journal.
- Select a special writing pen, color markers, paper, or notebook for use in journaling.
- Bring your journal with you to each class. In each class session different opportunities will be given to journal following various experiential exercises.